BOSTON RED SOX

BOSTON RED SOX

75th ANNIVERSARY HISTORY
1901-1975

Ellery H. Clark, Jr.

Foreword by
THOMAS A. YAWKEY, President,
Boston American League Baseball Company

An Exposition-Banner Book

EXPOSITION PRESS
HICKSVILLE, NEW YORK

CONTENTS

FOREWORD

As the Red Sox play in their 75th season, it seems quite appropriate that one of the most loyal Red Sox fans I have known through the years, Captain Ellery H. Clark, Jr., of the United States Naval Academy, should have his definitive ideas about the history of the Red Sox published.

Although the Red Sox have been supported loyally by millions of fans in the club's history, few have been any more dedicated than Captain Clark, who has spent countless hours in research, compiling the facts presented in this book. It has truly been a labor of love.

I'm sure all Red Sox fans will find this publication interesting and informative, and a valuable addition to the written history of the club.

Thomas A. Yawkey

THOMAS A. YAWKEY

ACKNOWLEDGMENTS

To all who have assisted in this project, the author's deepest appreciation, including the many Red Sox, retired and active, chronologically from Young through Yastrzemski, who so kindly provided oral and written documentary material, permission to use various facilities and sources, and to reproduce pictorial matter. In particular, credit is due the following, some of whom are deceased, yet still are very much in spirit with us:

Olympic Champion Ellery H. Clark, of Boston and Cohasset, Mass.: the author's father who early instilled in him an abiding faith in and dedication to the Red Sox
Boston Red Sox: Bill Crowley, Tom Dowd, and Barbara Tyler
William E. Clark: the author's son, who took many magnificent photographs
Captain Harry Hooper, Duffy Lewis, and Joe Wood, of the old World Champion Red Sox
The Sporting News and other Spink Publications: J. G. Taylor Spink and his son, current publisher, C. C. Johnson Spink; Chris Roewe and Paul MacFarlane, staff
The Baseball Magazine: Owner-editor Earl C. Noyes; later editor, Mac Grimmer
The MacMillan Company: Robert J. Markel, Executive Editor
Joe Cronin, Chairman of the Board, The American League of Professional Baseball Clubs
Editors and staff of Boston newspapers: The *Globe, Herald American, Herald Traveler, Post, Record American,* and *Transcript*

John Alden, Boston Public Library
Jim Bready, Baltimore *Sun*
George Carens, earlier the *Transcript*, later the *Traveler*
George Dearborn, Medford, Mass.
Mr. and Mrs. Howard J. Ehmke, Philadelphia, Pa.
Edward Lewis, Washington, D.C.
Charles Linehan, Belmont, Mass.
Bob McGarigle, Acton, Mass.
Arthur Sampson, the *Herald*
Dr. Vernon Tate, Annapolis, Md.
Marjorie Whittington, Annapolis, Md., secretary
Caroline Willis, Suggested Cover Design
Chip Waidner and Jonathan Waidner, grandsons who show
    excellent baseball talent and also maintain the Red Sox faith

Picture Credits

The following abbreviations identify the positions of the pictures on a page when two or more appear together: t = top; b = bottom; c = center; l = left; r = right. When all the pictures on a page are credited to a single source, only the page number is given, without position.

Baltimore *Sun:* 132*t*.
The Baseball Magazine: 73*t*, 75*t*, 79*b*, 80*t*, 98*t*, 99*t*, 100*b*, 101, 103*t*, 109*t*, 110*t* & *b*, 111, 112*t* & *c*, 130, 131, 133, 134*t* & *b*.
Hugh Bedient: 72.
Boston *Advertiser:* 103*c*, 104*t*.
Boston *Globe:* 112*b*.
Boston *Herald:* 66*b*, 76*t*, 80*b*, 106*t*, 107*c*, 109*c* & *b*, 140.
Trustees, Boston Public Library: 36, 38*b*, 74.
Boston *Record American:* 108*b*, 139.
Boston Red Sox: 97*t*, 134*c*, 135*t* & *c*, 136*t*, 142*c*, 143, 144*bl*.
Bill Clark: 129, 135*b*, 136*c* & *b*, 137, 138, 141, 142*t* & *b*, 144*br*, *tr*, & *tl*.
Clark Collection: 35, 37, 39*l*, 46*b*, 67, 68, 69*t*, 71*b*, 78*t* & *c*, 79*t*, 97*b*, 106*b*.
Dearborn Collection: 33, 38*c*, 40, 42, 43, 45, 46*t*, 47, 48, 65*t* & *b*, 66*t* & *c*.
Howard Ehmke: 107*t*.
Ira Flagstead: 107*b*.
Olaf Henricksen: 75*b*.
Harry Hooper: 76*b*.

Samuel Pond Jones: 105*b*.
Edward Lewis: 38*t*.
Marty McHale: 71*t*.
Carl Mays: 103*b*.
Mrs. Nat Niles: 41.
Buck O'Brien: 69*b*.
Official Base Ball Guide, 1902: 34.
Wally Schang: 104*b*.
Kip Selbach: 44, 65*c*.
The Sporting News: 70, 77, 78*b*, 99*b*, 100*t*, 102*t*, 105*t*, 106*c*, 108*t*,
    110*c*.
Harry M. Stevens, Inc.: 98*b*, 102*b*, 108*c*.
Ted Williams: 132*b*.
Joe Wood: 73*b*.
Cy Young: 39*r*

ESSENTIAL CHARACTERISTICS OF THE DEDICATED RED SOX FAN

INTRODUCTION

Several baseball writers over the years, though not including one from Boston, have expressed themselves on fringe areas of this important subject. Of course it cannot be explained fully in words, nor derived from a computer, but must to a degree be located on the far side of what the German poet Goethe meant when he affirmed, "There is a knowable and an unknowable." But, as an experienced Red Sox buff, the author hastens to rush in without angel benefit, and take a try at it. Operating on the premise it takes a Bostonian to know one, he examines forthwith some essential characteristics of this intriguing, unique species, of which he considers himself to be a reasonable, enduring specimen.

As in human fingerprints, no two qualified Red Sox fans are exactly alike, but they, as a breed, possess certain distinctive traits, of which some are particularly noticeable when they wear full seasonal plumage (such as either a straw hat with RED SOX on the ribbon or a blue cap properly adorned with white-bordered red B, for adults; with Red Sox shirts and similarly identified and labeled popcorn containers almost mandatory for teenagers and children). But they do not have to wave pennants, fortunately a dwindled practice since the 1903-1916 heyday of the Boston Royal Rooters.

All of us are familiar with and have our own definitions for such terms as patriotism, happiness, and the right thing. "Red Sox fan" naturally includes elements of all three as well as its own distinct connotations. It is variously a sports' religion, state of mind, requirement of life to those so possessed (there is no league with the devil, thus no exorcism is necessary or recommended), and one of the most mysterious yet satisfying expressions of this human condition. You either have it or you don't. It cannot be taught, learned, developed by special formula, or purchased by money or favor. Its qualities are born within the fortunate, often latent at first, and possibly aided by inheritance, should either parent be so endowed. Should both be, the prospects for Red Sox genes are exceedingly bright.

As in nature's powerful, unfailing semiannual command for waterfowl migration, so, too, does Fenway Park issue its seasonal, irresistible summons to those so possessed, many of whom at first do not realize their innate qualifications and eventual obligatory dutiful response. Thus, as hardy and enduring as the scoter species which twice a year course the Atlantic flyway, the annual migration of New England fans occurs, either physically or at least in spirit, to Fenway Park, from early April to October, sometimes well into October, should the season be a particularly rewarding one.

Between campaigns the faithful go into winter quarters, wherever they may be, regenerating themselves psychologically, quickly discarding the baseball misfortunes of the recent past with a *c'est la vie* attitude, and, should the previous campaign have been successful, increasingly becoming enthusiastic. Feeding eagerly on the February and especially March manna of the extensive New England press (the largest number of reporters to accompany any professional ball club), the fans usually believe the to-be-expected overly cheerful spring predictions. Twenty-game winners and .300 hitters freely are predicted. Meanwhile effective ticket-sale promotion has done well and the unwise fan who may wait until the last moment to buy tickets may find himself or herself on the outside, should the team be a contender.

By April's first week comes the relentless annual urge to Jersey Street, somewhat magical and clearly alluring. Already the favored few have attended spring training and the remainder of the flock are attentively restive, ready to respond to the call of the open ball park and the confined parking area.

And come they do! Although we now have an energy crisis, doubtless it will little affect spectator arrivals and departures when the team is home. But customarily in the past the true fans (women, men, teenagers and children) upon arrival by MTA, bus and private car into the Kenmore Square area, nimbly alighted. Then, afoot, and sometimes reminiscent of spawning salmon in their progress, frequently and of necessity jumping and leaping against the strong tide of heavy automobile traffic, they thrust their inevitable navigational way up the gradual street incline to Fenway Park, there to fulfill the homing instinct.

What are the most important traits of the true Boston fan? In the opinion of this author they are five: fortitude, loyalty, optimism, sportsmanship, and propagation of the Red Sox faith. Now, to each one.

1. *FORTITUDE.* This quality, hopefully accompanied by longevity, is an absolute necessity for the fan stoically and even somewhat gracefully to pass from peak to valley and, more pleasingly, to take the reverse course, as he or she follows the footsteps, sometimes staggering, of varying Boston fortunes. As we historically know, the temporary delightful peak of 1903-1904 was replaced by the equally temporary unhappy valley of 1906-1907, then the magnificent sustained heights of 1912-1918 were followed by the abysmal descent to the vast deep of 1922-1933. Later, the single tops of 1946 and 1967 were compensated

for by the intervening longish depression of 1959-1966. The fans' enduring fortitude, currently sensing fulfillment as perhaps was indicated by the recent (1969-1973) reasonable plateau, together with unfounded intimations of 1974 improvement, stimulated additional optimism. Undoubtedly, also in 1975!

2. *OPTIMISM, Part One.* Obviously a wonderful quality and attitude toward life, no matter what one's age, health and situation may be. The dedicated fan has a full measure of this. Facts and likelihood to the contrary, emotion and instinct toward the great accomplishment (at least a pennant, maybe both titles) leads the true supporter ever onward. To her or him there is no impossible dream. Wasn't that bit of falsehood demolished for all time by glorious 1967? The fan is a twentieth century modified Miguel Cervantes in her or his devotion to the ideal which, unlike Cervantes's, is the attainable and tangible League and World Championship.

The possessor becomes immune to unexpected or expected setbacks in this human life, blows which seemingly may be distributed without partiality, reason or even justification. There must be a relevancy, perhaps planned by the founding fathers, between the motto of Rhode Island (obviously a New England state and home of the number one Red Sox farm team) and this subject—Hope.

OPTIMISM, Part Two. Contrary to existing mythology, the loyal Red Sox fan is not a depressed, disturbed person seeking peculiar solace for his/her misfortunes, real or fancied, by accepting with defeatist pleasure the real or fancied misfortunes of the Boston team. No melancholia is a prerequisite, no disturbed psychical qualities of the still far-from-fathomed human soul are identified as characteristics of the species. If one evaluates the entire seventy-four-year scope of Red Sox history to date, of course mixed emotions can be identified; happiness, disappointment, frustration and satisfaction—perhaps more of two and three than one and four.

The perceptive, adjustable fan can and should take these in stride, thus learning from baseball a lesson that has been, is, and will be repeated in all phases and walks of the human experience. She and he have the opportunity of adjusting personal philosophy, or of reinforcing an already viable one, and to take serious note that the human spirit and state of mind constantly are subject to stress and strain. Such a sport as baseball is a microscopic revelation of the whole macrocosm of life in breadth. In that illuminating truth lies one of the greatest philosophic benefits of baseball and that is a desired contribution of this book to the sport's history. Records, statistics, emotions, anecdotes, pictures, and many other baseball-associated items all are important in their own right, but we must also attempt to put it all together and seek philosophically the significance to one's own individual life of baseball history and of fan participation in and evaluation of this. Perhaps, as in baseball, there are more losers than winners. But Boston fans always are optimistic!

3. *LOYALTY.* The true follower must have unwavering loyalty. When the team is at home, personal attendance is most worthy. Should this not be possible, then TV, radio and press communications are readily available, and watch-listen-read becomes the order of the day or night, dependent on the schedule.

The fan also is expected, even obligated by conscience, to support the team on the road, and again, the usual communications services do their part. Actually, to be there, of course, is best, and to this end frequent bus, train and plane special trips have been arranged in the past. Upon arrival at an alien park the fan must not show cowardice in a minority situation or blindly refuse equal rights and opportunities. He or she must stand up and be counted, especially in the top half of the symbolic seventh inning.

A few years ago, while in a hostile city, the author was performing this rite, as also was a group of six; three women and three men. Quickly they sped toward him, shook hands vigorously, then cited the great password, "We're from Boston, too!" This is the stuff of which sisterhood and brotherhood are made and provides a universal bond between Red Sox fans whether at home or on the road.

Root for the home team? Good God, yes, provided it's the Red Sox. In 1967 the author took the night train from Washington to Boston to be on hand for the first game of the Series. Detraining in the South Station he hastened to the nearest booth to buy Boston morning papers. Pinned to his lapel was his father's 1915 Boston Royal Rooters' World Series emblem; a miniature wool red sock surmounted by a large, round button bearing the single magical word BOSTON.

The lady in charge of the booth peered intently at this, then observed in a rich Irish brogue, "So, it's the Red Sox, is it? May the Saints be with Boston this day!" Though just a small anecdote and seemingly unfulfilled (they lost, 2-1), it was large in spirit; also so typical of the Boston population's rallying attitude in moments of athletic crisis. Certainly there were no signs of sophisticated, cynical indifference. A few hours later at Fenway, to the tune of "For Boston" (actually a Boston College football song), the team took the field, with this musical salute indicative of the mass support behind them.

Before the loyal but weary fan seeks daily rest in the sleep process, which Shakespeare so beautifully described as knitting the raveled sleeve of care, he or she must put in extra hours when the team plays on the coast, usually beginning around 11:00 P.M., Boston time. The game must be listened to from first pitch to final out. One does not have to qualify for such devotion to duty by suffering from insomnia or serving in a night-employment capacity, but these might help. Those who fall asleep are warned not to reveal such human weakness. They must know in their own hearts that this has been a lamentable transgression, hopefully repented and better still, never repeated, never acknowledged.

4. *SPORTSMANSHIP.* Although baseball technically is considered entertainment rather than a business, there is no acceptance on or off the field of the compassionate Eton philosophy which places how the game is played far above the results. Everybody knows in real professional life it is just the other way around. Nobody loves a loser except another loser and one need only consult the ever-growing list of dismissed managers and coaches to realize the harsh truth.

Our typical fan probably is more oriented toward Red Sox victory, however dull or exciting the game may be, rather than toward enjoying the merits of great plays in a losing encounter. This author opposes the hurling of insults and more tangible objects at any player, home team or visitor. But he heartily endorses applause at an opponent's good play, especially if it meets the qualification of not hurting the Boston cause. Exceptional visitor achievements, such as a no-hitter, deserve fullest recognition, even if "the team" has been done in.

Unfortunately there is an increasing tendency of grandstand and bleacher "managers" audibly to knock the home team or certain players on it, as in the cases of former players Ted Williams and Reggie Smith. But mature thought reveals this is not helpful. Few outspoken fans have a high boiling point, they speak almost before they think, some with beverage assistance. In accepted practice, when they bought their ticket they also purchased the right of free speech at the ball game, including insulting remarks. It is condoned by the establishment. This author disqualifies such a "fan" and does not identify him as belonging to the type of genuine fan he is evaluating in this article. Note the male, not female, reference to the unpleasant spectator.

5. *PROPAGATION OF THE SPECIES.* In general, the real fan, dependent on conditions, abilities, circumstances, be the individual a man or woman, is relied upon to propagate the species, otherwise it will become extinct, an unthinkable thought.

Children must be begotten, then reared the "right way," which of course means to support "the team" (Boston) in due course. Occasionally in the past there have been doubts about the wisdom of propagation, either of fans or ball players.

For example, when the author was a Boston lad of fifteen and had dreams that just maybe he might be a major league pitcher some day, he wrote a letter to a then famous National League player (mid 1920s) for some practical advice. He got it, but not from whom he had expected. Three weeks later, a reply arrived, written and signed by his wife. It read in part:

Dear Master Clark:
    May I suggest, should you decide to become a baseball player, that you remain single. Living with the boys these days [it was a near-cellar team] is rather difficult. . . .

However, for the truly dedicated prospective ball player, interested in statistical analysis of the past, he may wonder, in planned or unplanned parenthood in which of the American states eventual big league players most frequently have been born. These appear to be, though not necessarily in this order, Massachusetts, New York, Pennsylvania, Ohio, Illinois, and California, with recent inputs from Latin America. Thus, a wise child who favors stats intelligently will select parents living in one of these states, or in a Latin American country.

CONCLUSIONS. Fortitude, optimism, loyalty, sportsmanship, and propagation have been identified and discussed as significant characteristics of the dedicated Red Sox fan, be the individual man, woman, teenager, or child. Although, as discussed, philosophic and therapeutic benefits are available to all who so qualify, perhaps just a few so far have been aware of them, and might do some serious thinking as a result.

The fortunate are members of a captive audience, partly by instinct, partly by continuing choice. If one measures fan contentment loosely, by relating annual paid attendances and free listening to radio and TV to the yearly posture of the team, a somewhat glorious conclusion is reached, as evidence has indicated. It really doesn't matter whether the club is first or sixth, as long as a string of depressed seasons does not develop. Relevant statistics, both known and estimated, of the past forty years prove this truth.

Let the critics and unbelievers carp and shake heads at all this. What a wonderful state of mind for the fortunate, insulated against baseball and perhaps life's adversity and discouragement by these five characteristics, safe in their unshatterable cocoon. This author hereby recommends that the Boston City Council propose a resolution, since we are believers, as is Mrs. Ford, in equal rights and opportunities and heavenly influences, to change and broaden the city's Latin motto from *Sicut Patribus Sit Deus Nobis* to *Sicut Patribus et Matribus Sit Deus Nobis* (As God was with our fathers and mothers, so may He be with us). It is not irreverent to believe He, in His wisdom, has looked after and will continue to look after the Boston baseball fan, without restriction of sex.

So long as the Red Sox may continue, at least in spirit this author will always be with them. After all, it's spring again! Everybody knows the team will do better this year! 1974 was a fluke. Blame it on Watergate. Come on, Red Sox!

ANALYSIS OF PLAYER-SELECTED RED SOX GREAT MOMENTS

GENERAL INTRODUCTION. William Wordsworth, distinguished English poet, considered emotions recollected in tranquility appropriate and rewarding for author, reader and listener alike. The book's many illustrations offer occasional selected individual responses to this subject, in photo captions, of course relative to baseball, perhaps also to life in general. Some 40 Red Sox, former or present, contributed identifications and comments on their most thrilling, rewarding or satisfying memory as a Boston player. For the retireds, by coincidence there was an average of over thirty years between end of active career and completion of the question-answer process. Thus, ample time was provided for examination or possible reexamination by each one of them on this hitherto neglected research subject.

Since this documentary material is autobiographical and in certain instances quite soul-searching, there is no question as to its value in adding another dimension to the sphere of baseball, increasingly the subject of fresh viewpoints and broadening horizons. No such in-depth information previously has been gathered for interpretation in the literature of the sport or, indeed, any sport. The senior respondents now are deceased. In this newly yet quite belatedly probed area the author sought additional personal knowledge as to what degree, if any, at-the-time contemporary achievements later might have cooled, remained at the same approximate level, or even increased. Only the first assumption has proven negative.

The author, not being inclined toward or interested in exploring the unhappinesses of this life, deliberately did not venture through questions into the sad side of emotions, such as experienced in baseball by some Bostons and many others elsewhere in moments of athletic crisis, accompanied by defeat. But he believes, unsupported by evidence, the happy memories far outweigh the unexamined others. It also is quite likely that a minimum response would have been forthcoming to such research. Most people, regardless of whether someone thinks they should, dislike having past wounds, real or fancied, reopened. The scar of this painful area remains closed, generally speaking, and this is quite understandable.

Several significant general observations are possible, on the basis of substantial returns. Over 85 percent replied, proving Boston players' enthusiastic cooperation with this research-minded fan. Some of the lesser greats were extremely happy at being remembered years after they had hung up their equipment, and correspondence kept up until their deaths. Sustained great heroes, such as "Duffy" Lewis, Joe Wood, and the late Harry Hooper in particular, made the effort and time to respond frequently and in great, interesting detail, despite their continuing semiavalanche of general fan mail, much of it from youngsters wisely interested in the past. The author also gained fringe benefits, such as the memorabilia generosity of former players, their wives and widows. Photographically, such examples as the items donated by George Dearborn; the portraits of Selbach, O'Brien, and Ehmke presented by these individual athletes; the menu of Young's testimonial dinner to his Boston teammates, by Nat Niles's widow, are included.

Continuing, the author received, and responded accordingly

to, many requests from former Red Sox for individual or team pictures, since they had not retained any or had loaned ones which never were returned. Thus, interest in the past by one person rekindles it in another, and this bond of human companionship has been a most rewarding experience. The policy of enclosing stamped, self-addressed envelopes must have encouraged some to reply more promptly than otherwise because of not having a stamp or envelope, or both, handy at the moment.

SPECIFIC INTRODUCTION. Six conclusions on the respondents may be made before presenting an analysis of the actual answers. First, as a group, Red Sox longevity has exceeded that of the average American, perhaps a tribute in part to the general good physical-mental condition many have been fortunate in maintaining in later life. Second, almost every former player still retained an accurate, detailed memory; who was on base and in the field, what was the score, precise count, the type of pitch thrown, etc., as if these events were just occurring. Unlike an old track athlete the author once knew, who in later years had some pleasant failing of memory and, as a result, as his son commented, "He began winning races he really had lost," the reminiscent ball player does not violate actuality. Third, they all showed enduring respect for worthy opponents and admired success even if some of it had been at their own and team's expense. Fourth, back in the American League past and not distant past, when pitchers used to bat, they delighted in making occasional hits. Fifth, there was and is the All-Star Game importance to rookies so fortunate as to have been selected for such participation in their first full season. Last and most impressive, some in-depth perceptions and reflections were made on the importance of life and, by inference, its unity.

Data Background. We now tabulate, for readers' benefit, names of respondents, their playing years, when they replied, if retired, and interval between end of Boston career and completion of the question-answers.

Name	Boston Career	Year of Response	Interval (in years)
Collins	1901-1907	1930	23
Selbach	1904-1906	1954	48
Gibson	1903-1906	1956	50
Dinneen	1902-1907	1950	43
Parent	1901-1907	1953	46
Young	1901-1908	1953	45
Tannehill	1904-1908	1951	43
O'Brien	1911-1913	1955	42
Bedient	1912-1914	1960	46
Wood	1908-1915	1974	59
Carrigan	1906-1916	1950	34
Henriksen	1911-1917	1959	42
Janvrin	1911-1917	1950	33
Lewis	1910-1917	1974	57
Mays	1915-1919	1965	46
Schang	1918-1920	1954	34
Hooper	1909-1920	1974	54
McInnis	1918-1921	1950	29
Jones	1916-1921	1952	31
Menosky	1920-1923	1950	27
Ehmke	1923-1926	1956	30
Flagstead	1923-1929	1929	None
Cramer	1936-1940	1974	34
Cronin	1935-1945	1974	29
Ferriss	1945-1950	1955	5
Doerr	1937-1951	1955	4
Pesky	1942-1952	1974	22
DiMaggio	1940-1953	1970	17
Dobson	1941-50; 1954	1960	6
Parnell	1947-1956	1974	18
Williams	1939-1960	1954	None
Jensen	1954-1961	1970	9
Runnels	1958-1962	1965	3
Monbouquette	1958-1965	1974	9
Malzone	1955-1965	1974	9
Stange	1966-1970	1974	4
Lonborg	1965-1971	1974	3
Fisk	1969-	1974	None
Petrocelli	1963-	1974	None
Yastrzemski	1961-	1974	None

Analysis of Information. Somewhat arbitrarily counting Yaz equally classifiable as outfielder and first baseman, thus accomplishing some fractional totals, of the 40 respondents, 17 were pitchers, three catchers, 10½ infielders and 9½ outfielders. One cannot avoid the probable truth that thinking pitchers also enjoy writing! The returns are compiled under four categories: significant miscellany, pitching, batting, and fielding. There was almost equal numerical distribution within the pitching-batting-fielding replies, but the miscellany group easily was the most numerous.

1. *Significant Miscellany.* Included are: Hooper's 1912 Series religious experience (quoted in detail later); companionship with and admiration for fine groups of teammates in different periods of Red Sox history (Dinneen, Carrigan, Ferriss and Lonborg); appreciation of the great club effort in 1967 by Yastrzemski and Jim Lonborg. In the latter's words, "I was the winning pitcher, had been carried on the shoulders of some of America's finest fans and was able to share a moment in history with a group of people who so deserved the honor of being American League champions."

Earlier, in 1930, during the depths of the Great Depression, Manager-Captain Jimmy Collins had written the author from his Buffalo residence, with obvious poignancy, "In contrast to the present, those really were the good days when I led Boston to its first World Championship."

Also appreciation of Mr. Tom Yawkey (Cramer); of Boston fans' sportsmanship (Jones and Stange); of the fans' night given in his honor (Doerr); praise of Williams's 1958 bat prowess although it cost him (Runnels) the individual championship, and Williams's recognition of Eddie Collins's early influence upon his subsequent career. Adding further stature to the appreciation of Ted was Joe Cronin's statement. "My most pleasant Red Sox memory was Ted Williams getting 6 hits out of 8 times at bat on the last day of the 1941 season to raise his average over .400. Ted was hitting below .400 going into the double-header [against the Athletics] but he was so determined to accept the challenge." This is included under significant miscellany rather than batting because Mr. Cronin showed so much characteristic modesty about his own outstanding career, and such appreciation of one of his star player's well-earned highest honors. Continuing, Ehmke's emotional relief (1923) on leaving Detroit and the unpleasant situation he had experienced with Cobb; and both Malzone's (1957) and Fisk's (1972) many-faceted reactions at having been rookie participants in All-Star Games.

Harold Janvrin remarked to the author, "My inspiration to become a Red Sox player really began when I was at Boston English High, and so admired your Olympic Champion father [Ellery Clark, of the Boston Athletic Association] and his many-faceted athletic abilities." Hal later sent the author an autographed photo of himself as a Red Sox, with the marvelous inscription: "An autograph at my age? Hell!" Most interestingly when "Leaping Mike" Menosky replied to the author's inquiries, his best recollection was:

> My most pleasant Red Sox memory was meeting the many youngsters who hung around the players' gates at the American League parks, because it gave me a feel for the happiness and unhappiness of many boys. After I played my last game for Boston I became a parole officer in the Detroit District Court system and spent many years working with unfortunates on skid row. If I helped save one out of ten then this has been the most rewarding memory of my life to date, and the earlier association with young people when I was a ball player, including my 4 years with the Red Sox, played a part in this.

Of all the above commentaries, Hooper's is the most worthy of attention. With his very kind permission, these are his exact words. The situation: beginning of final and decisive 1912 World Series game at Fenway Park, between Boston and New York, each with three victories:

> When I was going out to my position in right field at

the start of the 8th game I saw a small piece of paper on the grass. I picked it up to get it out of the way. Then I saw it was a picture of the Sacred Heart of Jesus, with a little prayer. I read the prayer as I went out to my position. I asked Jesus if it was His will to let us win and I made a resolution to receive the Sacraments at first opportunity. Then I put the picture in the pocket of my pants.

It can easily be explained. Some fan dropped the picture, hoping I would find it. Larry Doyle [whose potential home run, which would have won the championship for New York, was turned into a spectacular out] was probably just as worthy as I, so why should I be aided at his expense?

But the way I caught the ball [see photograph, page 76] —how I was in the exact spot and position to catch it and how I caught it was as if someone had placed it in my hand. Then I jumped the [temporary] fence without crashing into someone who could have been badly hurt. Never lost my feet. All this has made me wonder ever since.

2. *Pitching.* Among these recollections: Young's ability to place fine performances on a level well above victory or defeat, when he coequally evaluated his 1904-perfect game and the 20-inning loss the next season, both against Waddell; Wood's nipping off Giants's rally in 1912 Series' first game; Bedient's win over Mathewson, also brilliant 0.50 ERA in same Series; Mays volunteering and accomplishing victory on road, at St. Louis; Dobson's 1946 Series perfect ERA against the Cardinals; and Monbouquette's realizing it might be his night before beginning his 1962 no-hitter. Parnell described his 1956 no-hitter as follows: "I do recall having a good sinker and throwing it about eighty percent of the time. During the game I really never did reach a state of nervousness. I feel the reason for that was because I just didn't expect it to happen. A few of my team-mates showed signs of being nervous mainly because they feared

making a bad play and messing up the no-hitter." Obviously all were outstanding achievements and remained etched in the achievers' memories.

3. *Batting.* Although a pitcher, Gibson minutely remembered his 1904-long sacrifice fly (almost a triple) off Chief Bender, who usually outsmarted him, but not on that occasion. Mays also recalled a game-winning hit. Others were: Henriksen's pinch double in final game of 1912 Series (later DiMaggio mentioned his two-bagger which also tied the score, this time in last encounter of 1946 Series); Lewis topping both clubs in World Series batting, 1915 and 1916; Pesky's game-winning homer on an opening day of the early 1940s; Jensen's 1959 "retirement" homer; Yaz's 1967 triple crown; and Petrocelli's two home runs in sixth game of 1967 Series. As might be expected of those so fortunate as to have participated in the World Series, these games were judged of far greater significance than those of the regular campaigns.

4. *Fielding.* Appreciative pitchers Tannehill and O'Brien, even after over forty-two years, each remembered with gratitude the encouragement and great defensive plays of their infields. Other selections: Parent's excitement, still high after forty-six years, of having been shortstop in Young's perfect game; Selbach's running catch some weeks later in 1904 which insured Boston the pennant; Schang's at-the-plate putouts in 1918 Series; McInnis's almost perfect (.999) 1921 fielding; and Flagstead's three-time demonstration in one 1926 game of double plays, cutting down base runners who had underestimated his catch-and-throw abilities. Indeed, great moments!

Conclusions. Believing this to have been a reasonable sampling over a considerable number of years and also convinced that these materials are fully capable of supporting valid conclusions, the author endorses the thinking reader to draw his or her own evaluations. Only one philosophic author-comment is offered. How valuable and wonderful it is to have on record such great moments and to learn how and probably why they have endured through the decades. It appears human experience survives the actual, limited time capsule of the moment of attainment. These accomplishments, probably excellent working examples of Ernest Hemingway's concept of grace under pressure (but not permeated with any of the philosophic aura of defeat which so engrossed the novelist), appear to have become suspended in the attentive minds of the attainers-beholders, at least for the remainder of their lifetimes.

The author feels privileged to have shared indirectly in this philosophic experience and will attempt to equate it with known great moments of people in other areas of the human condition. There is no end to these great moments, speaking of life broadly, and in the mind of the intent, perhaps equally so of the relaxed participant or observer there well may be a vague recognition of a unified pattern throughout human life, although quite probably beyond mankind's comprehension. Perhaps Hooper sensed this universality when he wrote, quoted previously, "It was as if someone had placed it in my hand." Whatever the reader's own interpretation may be of Hooper's philosophy, from the batter's point of view, both then and later in life, Doyle (whose general nickname was "Laughing Larry") paid generous, gracious tribute to the catch while also identifying his own personal misfortune. The term universality well may include the necessity of diverse human experiences, including in the athletic world, sometimes unpleasant and quite impossible for humans to fathom. Doyle's and Hooper's experiences and reactions, a fascinating study in opposites, yet with some strains of parallelism, adds credence to this theory.

THE ORIGINAL BALL PARK. Boston Americans in action at the Huntington Avenue Grounds. Separated from the nearby National League park by tracks of the New Haven Railroad, this was team's home, 1901-1911. Today, site of the grounds is occupied, quite fittingly, by the Physical Education Center of Northeastern University. Commemorative plaque was dedicated May 16, 1956, with club's original shortstop Fred Parent a distinguished guest.

1—McKenna; 2—Freeman; 3—Hemphill; 4—Parent; 5—Cuppy; 6—Young; 7—Kane; 8—Dowd; 9—Stahl; 10—Ferris; 11—Criger; 12—Collins, Capt.; 13—Schreckenghost; 14—Mitchell; 15—McLean. **1901** *Photo by Bachrach & Bro*

BOSTON AMERICAN LEAGUE BASE BALL CLUB.

EAGER BOSTONIANS WELCOMED BASEBALL EXPANSION! Bachrach put the lens on the original Boston Americans, who took the field in April, 1901, first season of the then new American League. A strong contender, club finished second (79-57) to champion Chicago. Kane and McKenna never played a game for Boston; McLean made first pinch hit in League. Two Boston caps on floor were not symbolic of team's early fortunes; they would win two pennants in first four years.

A 1901 REPRESENTATIVE AT-HOME SCORECARD (pronounced "skohcahd" in Boston). Under persuasive leadership of Manager-Captain Jimmy Collins, renowned third baseman (1896-1900) of the senior Boston Nationals, four teammates joined the new club; outfielder Chick Stahl (.326), first baseman Buck Freeman (.301), pitchers Parson Lewis (78-47) and George Cuppy (8-4). Great battery of Cy Young (286-169) and Lou Criger (.261) was obtained from the St. Louis Nationals.

BOSTON.	1	2	3	4	5	6	7	8	9	10	AB	R	1B	TB	SH	PO	A	E
Dowd, l f	8							8										
Stahl, c f	7					9		III										
Collins, 3 b	1-3						2	6-3										
Freeman, 1 b					0		9	ap										
Hemphill, r f	7				6-3		6-3	6-3										
Parent, s s	6-3							F6										
Ferris, 2 b			⓪			III		BB										
Criger, c					6-3			1-3										
Lewis, p								3										
TOTAL HITS.	0			0		0	0	1										

35

NO LONGER THE PRACTICE. 1903 Series participants fraternally posed for this team-team picture, obviously with the home club well situated in front, possibly an indication of how the teams would finish. Note typical Boston Police Department uniforms of the day in background. Although the Pirates lost athletically, financially their individual pleasure exceeded that of their conquerors because their shares were larger, a Series oddity that has not been repeated.

RAREST 1903 FIRST WORLD SERIES SCORECARD. In 1903 the team raced to its first American League pennant (91-47) outdistancing runner-up Philadelphia by 14 1/2. Pictured rival managers are in baseball Hall of Fame. "Nuff said" Mike McGreevy was prominent Columbus Avenue saloon proprietor. This was the period when baseball's greatest partisans gathered in the sawdust-strewn, stomach-filling, free lunch bars for the exchange of conviviality, baseball knowledge, preference, wit, and humor.

PITTSBURGH (then spelled Pittsburg) WON THIS THIRD SERIES GAME AT BOSTON, 4-2. But the original Series required five victories and even though the Pirates won three of first four, Boston zoomed back with four straight. Boston's winning player shares each amounted to $1,182, as pitching depth (Dinneen and Young over Deacon Phillippe) prevailed. Note dollar-a-quart whiskey ad in scorecard.

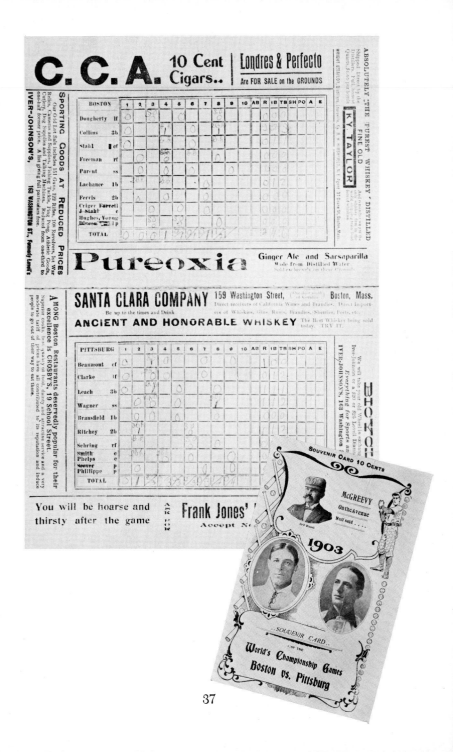

PITCHER LEWIS OF THE BOSTON AMERICANS.

EDWARD "PARSON" LEWIS. 16-17 in 1901, his only year with the club, earlier (1898) had been champion pitcher (Boston Nationals) in the senior League. Well educated, with two degrees from Williams, later an outstanding president of the University of New Hampshire; he and Robert Frost, the great American poet, were close friends and shared mutual interests in baseball and poetry. Lewis kept a valuable diary during playing days with both Boston teams. In it he noted after one of his 1901 appearances, "Give many bases on balls. . . . Too much pitching with the feeling 'I hope it goes over' and too little 'It can't help go over.' Same confidence secret of success in batting, in fielding a ball, in spitting into a spittoon, in public speaking, in shaving."

GLORY TO BOSTON! Substantial emblem of victory, this huge World Champion flag (first of five to date) is smartly hoisted to top of Huntington Avenue Grounds' flagpole by Manager-Captain Jimmy Collins, with equally proud teammates standing by. Not many, on the field or in the stands on this occasion in early 1904, would predict in the same year that although Boston would repeat their championship, the National League winner would refuse to meet them. This led to some people unofficially declaring the Hub team World Champions by default, or continuation.

ONCE A SPORTSMAN, ALWAYS A SPORTSMAN. So great was Boston's hero worship at the time that a man who had shaken the hand of a man who had shaken the hand of John L. Sullivan was said not to have lived in vain. The "Boston Strong Boy," ten years earlier the World Heavyweight Boxing Champion, discusses aggressiveness with Manager Collins. Gentleman Jim Corbett, who had dethroned John L., and also a baseball fan, attended two of the Series games.

"CY" YOUNG NUMBER

THE
BASEBALL
MAGAZINE

SEPTEMBER
1908

Printed All Water

How I Learned
to Pitch"
By "CY" YOUNG

PRICE
15 CTS.

BOSTON GROUND
NEW YORK LEAGUE TEAM

Cy Young

Newcomerstown, Ohio
October 6, 1953

Ellery Clark!:

The biggest thrill
was the Perfect game against
the Athletics. also the 20 ing
game. Both games against athletics
and Rube Waddell was the
pitcher.

Cordially

Cy Young

Young's Perfect Game, May 5, 1904

The season of 1904 was famous for the many brilliant pitching duels involving Boston pitchers. On May 1, that impish child of nature, Rube Waddell, pitched a one-hit game against the Pilgrims at the Huntington Avenue grounds and won by a score of 3 to 2. Only two Boston batters reached base, as Jesse Tannehill, the left-hander, was the defeated Pilgrim boxman.

Waddell had a lot of fun crowing about his feat the next few days, and he unquestionably inspired Cy Young to pitching the classic of his brilliant career. He taunted Cy to face him, and shouted, "I'll give you the same what I give Tannehill."

The two met in the last game of the series in Boston, May 5, and it really showed what Young could do when he had his dander up. He retired the twenty-seven Athletics who faced him in order, one of the six perfect games of major league history. He reversed the former score, defeating Waddell, 3 to 0. "How did you like that one, you hayseed?" farmer Young yelled happily at the disgruntled Rube when it was over. It was Young's second no-hit game, as he had pitched his first with the old Cleveland Spiders of the National League in 1897.

Connie Mack was as much impressed with Young's victory as Collins was, and made no effort to hide it. "I never saw such a game pitched," said the tall man from Brookfield with unfeigned admiration. "He knew what he was doing with every pitch. Cy was perfect! Just perfect!"*

The Twenty Inning Game, July 4, 1905

The afternoon tilt was another memorable pitching duel between Young, by this time thirty-eight, and Rube Waddell, and the battle made conversation for Boston fans for weeks. The two pitching knights—the grand old right-hander and the king of southpaws, fought it out for twenty innings before Rube triumphed by a score of 4 to 2. An error, a hit batsman, two hits, and a force play finally gave the Athletics their winning runs.

Perhaps the most remarkable thing about the game was that Young went through the entire twenty innings without giving up a single base on balls, though in the twentieth inning an inside pitch hit Jack Knight, the young Philadelphia shortstop, on the head, knocking him unconscious. Losing the game after that near-perfect control really vexed the old fellow.

"I don't walk anybody in twenty innings, and I still lose," said Cy. "Well, I'll be damned!"

Young gave up eighteen hits to fifteen for Waddell, and after Boston scored twice in the first inning, the Rube turned back the Pilgrims scoreless for the next nineteen frames. Harry Davis tied it for the Athletics when he smacked Young for a sixth-inning home run.

"Talk about box work—Young and Waddell never did better work," enthused Frederic O'Connell. "And some folks say that Young is all in. If they had only seen him on July 4, they would change their opinion quickly and say he still is the G. O. M. [Grand Old Man]."*

THE INCOMPARABLE CY YOUNG. In relation to baseball, American art is much better known for cartoons than paintings. But this inspiring portrait, by Abbot H. Thayer of New Hampshire, now deservedly housed at Cooperstown, is a notable exception. Young (1901-1908) is win-ningest Red Sox pitcher to date, with 190-113. He almost literally inundated the record books. League leader in at least twelve seasonal departments, he still holds six Boston records. Cy completed 92 percent of games he started for Red Sox and in pennant, 1904, failed to finish only one.

YOUNG RECALLS HIS TWO GREATEST ACHIEVEMENTS. His value of his own best accomplishments transcended victory or defeat. As indicated, he selected one of each. He was thirty-seven at the time of the perfect game. In the 20-inning defeat of the next season his control was per-fect; not a single walk issued. Cy not only was genial, he was beloved. By pleasant coincidence, during his last season with the early Red Sox he was presented a large loving cup on August 13, 1908, inscribed "From the ball players of the American League, to show their appreciation to Cy Young as a man and as a ball player." Within the next month (see following photo-graphs), Young expressed his appreciation to his Boston teammates by a special dinner in their honor.

LOU CRIGER (1901-1908). Criger and Young were an exceptional battery; psychologically and professionally a perfect blend. Although Lou's bat mark was modest, he obtained his fair share of extra base hits and walks. Quick of reflexes, Criger had a strong arm and nimble feet, twice leading the League in fielding. Of the course of runs he scored for Boston in 1904, the most rewarding was the last, which gained the pennant in New York.

'CY' YOUNG, PITTED AGAINST "RUBE WAD
LETS NO ATHLETIC REACH FIRST BAS
10,267 SEE HIM CROWNED KING OF PITCHERS

MAY 5, 1904—THE PERFECT GAME. Boston cartoonist records his impressions of this classic at home against Philadelphia. In it, Cy Young fanned eight, ten flied out, nine were retired by the infield, as the Boston pitcher clearly showed great balance in his masterpiece. Pensive Connie Mack ultimately managed the Athletics for fifty seasons. Note lower left, and comment on left-handed batter versus left-handed pitcher, in which Freeman achieved the advantage.

Menu

BLUE POINTS, LAKE STYLE

GREEN OLIVES   WOOD'S CELERY   BRADY RADISHES

CONSOMMÉ À LA SULLIVAN

BOILED FRESH SALMON, CRIGER SAUCE
THONEY CUCUMBERS   NILES TOMATOES   KELLEY POTATOES

FRESH PUTNAM FARM CHICKEN, CY YOUNG STYLE
STAHL POTATOES   GESSLER JELLY

PLANKED SIRLOIN STEAK, AU DONAHUE DRESSING
ARELLANES FRITTERS   WAGNER GLACÉ
HIGGINS POTATOES   JERRY PEAS   LORD'S STRING BEANS

SPRING SALAD À LA BURCHELL

PLUM PUDDING, STEELE SAUCE

CICOTTE SUNDAE   CRAVATH CAKES
HOEY RAISINS   SPEAKER'S SALTED NUTS   CARRIGAN GRAPES

McMAHON'S CHEESE   McCONNELL'S CRACKERS
AMERICAN LEAGUE STYLE

MORGAN COFFEE   CIGARS

COMPLIMENTARY DINNER

GIVEN BY

CY YOUNG

TO THE MEMBERS OF THE

BOSTON AMERICAN BASE BALL CLUB

STUDENTS' SPA
PUTNAM HOUSE
BOSTON, MASS
SEPT. 15, 1908

COMING EVENTS CAST THEIR SHADOW BEFORE? Even off the field, and sometimes pleasantly Popular Cy, at end of his eighth Boston season, honored his teammates by "A Complimentary Dinner to the members of the Boston American Base Ball Club," on September 15, 1908, given at Put's (the Putnam House), the then famous ballplayers' hotel, near the old park. As indicated, each course or dish was labeled with a Red Sox player's name; Green olives were for the trainer, Charley Green; Jerry peas for mascot Jerry McCarthy; and blue points for Manager Fred Lake. Five months later, Young was traded to the Cleveland Americans.

41

NEARING THE END OF THE PENNANT RACE

SEASON 1904 PRODUCED THRILLING STRETCH DUEL. Artist Scott's cartoon obviously shows Boston nearing the flag, less obviously suggests the sun shining more in the direction of the defenders than New York. At home on October 8, the Collinsmen had taken two games, also the lead, with the final moment of truth scheduled in New York for concluding doubleheader. Boston needed one game; they were determined the return train trip would not seem a painful eternity, which happened after the 1946 World Series finale in St. Louis.

CHAMPIONSHIP BASEBALL

THE PENNANT WINNERS.

CESBRO PRESENTED WITH A FUR

THE PENNANT RUN FOR THE BOSTON'S

CRISIS SURMOUNTED!
As a New York cameraman recorded, and quite possibly not too happily, the Boston Champions won their second straight pennant on the road, prevailing in the decisive opener when Lou Criger sprinted in from third in the top of the ninth with what was to be the only run of the game.

Albert "Kip" Selbach
61 South Warren Avenue
Columbus 4, Ohio
January 5, 1954

Dear Mr. Clark:

I was very pleased to receive your letter. Yes, I do recall your father. Also, if you see Norwood Gibson, tell him "hello". I see Cy Young every now and then, but none of the others your letter mentioned. His eye sight is very bad now, you know; so he does not get to our house as often as he used to.

I was playing with Washington and was traded to Boston in 1904, in the Spring. Before that, I started out in 1893 and played two months in Chattanooga and was sold to Washington. I reported to Washington, in 1894, as a catcher. When I got there, they had three old catchers and did not have room for me in that position. I was tried out in the outfield and I showed up so well, they kept me there. I never caught a game in the Big League. I never played the Minor League for the whole season; nor did I ever play the bench. I played in every inning of every game played, unless I was hurt.

I recall an incident in the final game of the season. It was a double header. Two men were out and a man on third for New York. Elberfelt came to bat and hit a hard line hit over the shortstop. I came in fast from left and caught it knee high to end the game in Boston's favor. Previously, the pitcher, Chesbro, had thrown a spit ball and it got out of control and went wild over the catcher's head, scoring the winning run. This made us win the American League Championship, but the New York Nationals wouldn't play us for the World Series.

I am enclosing a picture taken after we won the championship in 1904. I will be eighty-two years of age March 24th, 1954.

I am also enclosing your envelope, as you may be able to use it further.

Thanking you again for your interest, I remain

Yours truly,
Al. Selbach

But Bill Dinneen was in trouble in the bottom of the ninth and this letter years later from Kip Selbach to the author vividly recalls his decisive catch which ended the pennant hopes of the gallant New York Highlanders. Some hours later joyous Boston fans greeted their heroes as they stepped off the train in the South Station, champions in every sense of the word.

"STUNTS" OF THE "CHAMPS" THAT HELPED WIN THE PENNANT

FERRIS PLAYED PHENOMENAL BALL

COLLINS EASY GOOD JUDGMENT WAS THE DELIGHT OF THE FANS

TANNEHILL AND YOUNG MADE NEW RECORDS AS TWIRLERS

LACHANCE NABBED EVERYTHING IN REACH

CRIGER IS A HUMAN BACK STOP

FREEMAN BECAME FAMOUS FOR HOME RUNS

STAHL PROVED HIS ABILITY AS CENTRE FIELDER

PARENT IS ONE OF THE BEST SHORT STOPS IN THE LEAGUE

SELBACK THE CRACK LEFT FIELDER

DUKE FARRELL ONE OF THE CRACK BOSTON BATTERIES AND COACHER

DINEEN, GIBSON AND WINTERS WHO MADE IT HOT FOR THE OPPOSING TEAMS.

Dowling

CHAMPS! Boston artist Dowling shows creativity in depicting 14 heroes of 1904. Baseball cartoonists were of great importance, especially in a period when newspapers had few photographs and the human interest relevance to readers best could be conveyed by drawings. In season 1904, Cy Young hurled 336 innings without relief, completed 41 out of 43 games started. Relief pitcher was an unknown term for years to come.

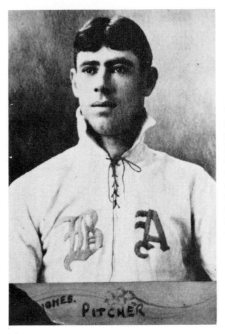

"LONG TOM" HUGHES (1902-1903). In his brief Boston career was 23-10, with 1903 his best contribution, at 20-7. The B A on Tom's shirt denoted Boston Americans, to distinguish them from the Boston Nationals. Players' sweaters had white buttons and an English-style B on left front. Boston Americans was the formal, official name of the team in this period, though early and nonenduring nicknames included Pilgrims and Puritans, which lacked the fan appeal of the later (1907) well-chosen Red Sox.

NORWOOD GIBSON (1902-1906). A Notre Dame college man, Norwood's best year was 1904, at 17-14, with career 34-32. In 1904 Young, Dinneen, Tannehill and he won 88 of Boston's 95 triumphs. He also enjoyed his batting. Against Chief Bender, as he later wrote, "He knew I was weak on a curve ball, that's what I looked for and got. I hit it up against the left field fence and batted in a run for Boston."

46

OPENING AT THE HUNTINGTON-AV GROUNDS.

THE FEELING THAT MAKES ALL MANKIND KIN—"PLAY BALL"

"ENJOY YOURSELF, IT'S LATER THAN YOU THINK!" Over-the-hill prospects to some did not appear likely in April, 1905, on Opening Day. But gone for eight years would be baseball supremacy, disappearing perhaps symbolically with Boston's chill east wind. In 1908-1911, the team would lose 484, win only 430. Note players' horse-drawn carriage. Hooper recalls of the 1911 club, "We used to enjoy whistling at and talking to the pretty Boston girls on the way to the park." Some pastimes, unlike vehicles, don't change!

47

GEORGE "CANDY" LACHANCE (1902-1905). Mustachioed first baseman and a dedicated consumer of candy, some of it from the then suburban nearby Walter Baker Chocolate Factory, George was a very talented fielder. In his first four Boston seasons he had an unusually high number of putouts; certain proof that Red Sox pitchers tended to keep their offerings low, thereby creating well above average infield opportunities.

PAT DOUGHERTY (1902-1904). An outfielder, was substantial Red Sox hitter in his first two seasons. In 1903, topped League in hits and runs. In the Series, became first player to crack two homers in one contest, the second, as well as leading both teams in total bases. His son-in-law is the distinguished soccer coach, Joe Palone, at the U.S. Military Academy.

ALBERT "HOBE" FERRIS (1901-1907). A rugged second baseman with a seven-year tenure, the longest in club's history until Bob Doerr. "Hobe" was very active and skillful afield, and at bat, he was the top Bostonian in 1903 Series RBIs. In this period of annual salaries in low five figures, a number of ball players, including at least one from Boston, augmented basic income with profits from abilities at such games of skill and chance as crap shooting and cards. Obviously, there were losers, too.

ANALYSIS OF
RED SOX SCORECARD
ADVERTISING, 1901-1974

Major League baseball audiences are partly voluntary, partly captive. One of the essentials to the average fan is a scorecard, wherein the lineups and the space provided for scoring is a necessity. But there is additional information of considerable direct baseball interest, such as pictures of and articles on home team players, selected stats, remainder of the schedule, next home games, ground and other rules. But whether a scorecard cost a nickel back in 1901 or thirty-five cents in 1974, the truth remains they do not pay for themselves by sales alone. They are made profitable by advertising.

Although baseball is classified as an entertainment, we all realize success on the field is the more frequent measurer, as managers well know. Advertising standards likewise are in tune with success, or expected success, and deposed executives in this area correspond to dispensed-with managers, however just or unjust such personnel changes may have been. There is fierce competition in the scorecards for potential customers of merchandise and services. Advertisers also have their pennant winners, though only they themselves possibly, rather than probably, know what the actual results have been. There are no available published advertising "gate" figures, such as baseball has, directly related to scorecards to indicate this factor.

Perhaps the general advertising premise has been and continues to be one of volume exposure and repetition. For example, in the period 1967-1974, average annual Red Sox attendance has been over a million and a half people. Even making allowances for repeaters and to a degree for children, the volume of readers and potential customers is there, and one of the best in years. Every effort made by the public relations department of the home team and the advertisers to make the best possible scorecard is most important, because it is essential to the advertisers that the programs be read and preferably retained and carried home for further consultation and action. Obviously there are certain choice pages and sections located within the program which are considered better than others in their potential appeal to the reader and the frequency with which they will be noticed. Some of these are: outside and inside front cover, inside and outside back cover, and those in the center which present the opposing lineups. More about these later.

It seems reasonable to devote one essay in this series to the subject in an attempt to discover patterns and trends of Boston advertising, to see which products endure and which do not, and which are of special interest for one reason or another. To this end the author, from his personal collection, has examined in detail some twenty-five representative Red Sox programs of the period considered. He knows this has not been a previously explored area, either for Boston or any other team. It also may be generally representative of all other big league baseball programs, with certain parochial Boston differences and flavors, as will be presented in due time.

From the advertisers' point of view, the potential customer must be influenced to buy, by producing reader conviction, "I've got to have this or that or consume this or that or do this or that." If the ad has sufficient irresistible appeal, the fan will not draw up distinctive separative lines between necessity and luxury. Desire and the pocketbook combined will make the decisive decisions. To those also interested in the sociological history of our country, the following "yellow pages" list of classified baseball advertising, arranged by the author, will cover the vanished past, the enduring past, the newer interests, including, of course, the reflection of changing technology as well as customs. Let us begin with the disappeared ads, though their subjects generally have not gone with the passing scene. Some flourish, such as bowling, tours, and burlesque (chiefly canned and an extension of the original), others may take a bit of searching to locate.

Arranged alphabetically, these include: amusement parks, billiards, bowling, burlesque, unfermented champagne, Aunt Mary's cough syrup, private detectives, dermatologists, Old Grist Mill dog bread, aid for tired feet, garters, laundry, marshmallows, messenger boys, pianos, relief from piles, plastic surgeons, pool, poultry dressing, Dr. Swett's Original Root Beer, saloons, soap, suspenders, talking machines, Symphony Hall Pops, "Bull" Durham tobacco, tours, Turkish baths, umbrellas, undertaker, union suits, and vaudeville.

Middle-aged to relative newcomers, obviously showing trends of recent times, alphabetically include: air lines, Army R.O.T.C., banks (markedly increased in number), baseball summer camp (Lakeville), Data Forms Co., Inc., department stores (increased), Fenway Park Painters, gasoline, Gino's, Jimmy Fund (Ted Williams is of great service to this children's cancer research and facilities organization), junior colleges, Marlboro coffee, Massachusetts Turnpike, McDonald's, Navy Recruiter, newspapers (markedly increased), TV stations (ditto), United Way, Vodka (Old Mr. Boston, of course; who else would be appropriate in the Hub?), Wax Museum (no, the old, slow fielders are not there!), and the Yellow Pages. No question, but the breadth of services and merchandise is far greater than in the early Red Sox days, and the hardy perennials continue.

Over the years the most frequent, enduring ads have been

for ale, automobiles, banks, beer, chocolates, cigarettes, cigars, frankfurts, mustard, newspapers, popcorn, potato chips, razors, restaurants, soft drinks (Coca-Cola in particular), and whiskey/ whisky (variously spelled). The actual top ten leaders by volume of advertising have been: cigars, cigarettes, whisky, beer and ale, hotels, restaurants, men's clothing, soft drinks, ice cream, and insurance. These statistics clearly should be of interest to contemporary advertisers who well might be guided for the future in part by what the past pattern has been. Seven are consumables, one provides shelter, another clothing, and the tenth provides family and associated security in an insured's case of death.

We now examine ten selected ads of special interest, one of which most unfortunately was in cruel and unfair taste though probably not so identified by whoever prepared the ad and authorized its publication; the author censures the affair.

1. *Anti-suffrage.* In a 1915 scorecard ad, signed by the Women's Anti-Suffrage Assoc'n of Boston, a No vote in the election of November 2, 1915, was recommended and justified on the thesis, "For the protection of your Women who do not wish to be forced into politics." Nevertheless, some five years later the Nineteenth Amendment was adopted on August 26, 1920.

2. *Ethnic Slur.* On the outside back cover of the 1903 card was an ad for a Boston-made soap, with accompanying sketch showing an open-jawed crocodile emerging from a river onto a beach, and rapidly approaching an unsuspecting, crawling black child. The caption read, "For the removal of discolorations."

3. *Two Early Leaders.* Schlitz, "the beer that made Milwaukee famous," was the first ad in its field, 1901, appropriately the same season when Milwaukee had a team in the League. Coca-Cola took first honors in the soft drink competition, initially appearing in 1903, priced at a nickel a glass.

4. *Three-Day Method.* Quite probably some kind of an antecedent of Alcoholic Anonymous, at least in intention, a doctor advertised in the 1912 World Series program his ability to cure the drink habit by destroying the craving for liquor within the stated limited period. A testimonial letter from a former "jolly good fellow" accompanied the message.

5. *1912 Not a Complete Year of Boston Joy.* Although the Red Sox won both the League championship and World Series, City Hall had its problems. In a paid ad, signed by the Boston Tax Collector, and ominously headed "Delinquent Taxpayers Last Notice," addressees were informed that unpaid personal and poll taxes would result in a prompt visit by the constable. The warning ended with the uncheery words, "He will surely come; he will not tarry."

6. *Loss of Ruth Somewhat Mitigated?* In a 1920 card of a game in which Babe Ruth played left field for the Yankees and batted third, on the page following the New York lineup the reader was urged to smoke a Babe Ruth cigar, claimed to be the best one made in Boston and his greatest hit. By inference to the philosophic Red Sox smoker, the player might be gone, but the associated aroma lingered on. So did Ruth's. The Babe had a financial interest in the product.

7. *Ladies' Days.* Although program advertising in general clearly did not direct its attention to women, this was an exception. One of 1916 stated, "An acceptable gift to any lady would be a 25 game book to Grand Stand at $12.50." Even in terms of extensive purchasing power and limited prices of that time, at fifty cents a game, and to see a World Champion team at that, this was a great opportunity, to say nothing of the chauvinistic male impression made on the lady.

8. *Private Detectives.* With the implication that a baseball buff's indirect eye might well be elsewhere than at the ball park during unfortunate personal situations, there were a number

of ads for "private eye" service, such as in 1910, which had an ominous futuristic ring about them; "Family troubles, alienation and abduction cases solicited."

9. *Entertainment in Different Places for Different Tastes.* In 1910, burlesque at Waldron's Casino and the next year the same kind of attraction was featured at the Gaiety, both second only to the unrepresented Old Howard. On the other side of town, very accessible to the old ball park (also to the later Fenway) the world famous Boston Symphony Pops was advertised, also in 1911, with available on-the-floor best seats at seventy-five cents.

10. *Talk About Bargains!* Typical buys of yesteryear: bicycles at $13.00 (1901); Kodak Brownies at $1.00 (1904); Uncle Dudley cigars at five cents (1901); suits at $15.00 (1901); hotel rooms, single occupancy, at seventy-five cents (1901); Gem razors at $1.00 (1923); Hotel Somerset lunches at seventy-five cents (1914); Climax plug tobacco at ten cents a tin (1920); Waltham watches at $8.80 (1913); Taylor's whiskey at $1.00 per quart (1901 and later); "Bull" Durham tobacco—two bags made 100 cigarettes if you rolled your own—for fifteen cents (1912); and straw hats at $2.00 (1912).

Over the years, cigars have maintained a slight numerical lead over cigarettes with the historical background advantage of being popular sooner than the later-comers. The first cigar ad appeared in the 1901 scorecard while one for cigarettes—and an Egyptian brand at that—was not printed until a year later. In the first sixteen years of Red Sox scorecards, cigarettes trailed cigars by a 1-3 ratio, which has become much closer since that time. However in this same period, and almost as tight as the 1908 American League pennant race (1½ games separated the first three teams), was the finish between cigars (19), whisky (18), and ales and beer (17), proving that when there is smoke, there also are intoxicants! But if one should pool the latter two, the wet look would prevail, and tobaccos would be contesting for a distant second place. This leads to the subject of "Bull" Durham.

It pays to advertise and to advertise, one pays, at least in the scorecard of a professional baseball club. "Bull" Durham tobacco originated in 1859, some ten years before the appearance of the famous Cincinnati Red Stockings, undefeated in their first season, and seventeen years prior to formation of the National League. In a full-page ad in the Red Sox 1912 World Series program, the company announced 1911 results, in which the extent both of their product and American professional baseball was amazing. In 1911 the company paid a total of $11,900 to 238 batters in professional leagues fortunate enough "in a regularly scheduled Baseball game . . . [to have] hit the big cut-out 'Bull' Durham sign that stands in nearly every ball park, with a fairly batted fly ball." 238 $\times$ $50 (the award promised) =$11,900. Speaker of Boston was one.

4,133 professional ball players of that season made home runs, of which the total home run productivity for the National and American Leagues had been exactly 510. This meant that major leaguers had accounted for only 12 percent of the entire homer production. Therefore, nonmajors' professionals accomplished the other 88 percent, indicating the great number as well as wide geographic distribution of other professional leagues and teams in a period of American history when baseball indeed was the national pastime, unassailed by football, basketball, and hockey. Further, the company presented each home run hitter with seventy-two five-cent bags of their product; and they announced the total weight of these amounted to exactly 18,598½ pounds, an awful lot of "Bull." There is no doubt that "Bull" Durham was by far the best known of the tobaccos of the period, at least from the point of view of the players. Of coincidental interesting advertising comparison, but of course well to seaward of scorecards, was Sir Thomas Lipton's gift of a pound of his tea to each crew member of the world-cruising American battleship squadron in 1907-1909.

We now proceed to the most favored advertising positions in scorecards. Mentioned earlier, there were and are certain preferred scorecard locations for advertisements, of which four survive; inside front cover, centerspread, inside and outside back cover. Before the Boston front outside cover was barred for advertising other than of the home team, Osgood's home furnishings first appeared, 1901, in this position. Neapolitan Ice Cream and Dr. Swett's Original Root Beer were first whole-page tenants in inside front and back covers, respectively. In contrast, these latter positions in recent years generally have seen cigarettes and liquors the keepers. As to the center spread, except for one year, numerous small advertisements have vied for attention and space. But back in the 1916 World Series program, Dodge Motor Company completely dominated the area, with four of their cars illustrated, one each, above and below the rival teams' lineups.

Prohibition did not put a crimp in Boston scorecard advertising, strange as it may seem to many readers. The facts were these. In the early years of the club, liquor ads were plentiful, but when we approach the immediate years before the Act, and we are in the World War I period, the size of the scorecards for various reasons shrank back to what it had been the first season; namely, two pages. But regardless of size, liquor appearances were very few. In brief, the analysis shows few before the Act, of course none during its existence, and no great influx immediately after.

On special occasions, such as in the 1967 World Series program, loyal Boston, New England, and national concerns paid very warming tributes in their ads to the great accomplishment of the 1967 American League Champions, an indication that business has a heart and can reflect the great mass appeal the fighting Red Sox of that year achieved.

In more recent seasons, with an obvious connection between TV and other sponsors and the scorecard, there has been an interesting pattern of large ads. For example, in 1974 programs, inside front and back covers went to Lechmere Stores, outside back to Marlboro cigarettes, and center strips divided between two banks, two newspapers, TV-radio, Narragansett Beer, and an auto dealer. Full pages were taken by a variety of advertisers and their wares; two pages by Jordan Marsh Company, single ones by Coca-Cola, Red Sox tickets, Holiday franks, the Massachusetts State Lottery, the MTA, Gillette, Salem, Camel, and Winston cigarettes, Old Smuggler Scotch, and O.F.C. Canadian whisky. At thirty-five cents a program, the fifty-six-page production is a bargain because of combined baseball-advertising content. Much program credit is due Bill Crowley.

Not incidentally, H. M. Stevens, Inc., Fenway Park concessionaires continuously since 1916, publish the program in four annual editions, reporting in 1974 an audited average annual program circulation of 426,516 and cumulative readership estimated at approximately two million per year. Boston, area, and national advertisers continue to try to attract the attention of the Red Sox "baseball crowd" and hopefully to make lifetime customers of them. Certain consumables, assuming they are not brought into the park by customers, have the inside track, and these are sold by H. M. Stevens, Inc. But since only a few hours a day or week are spent at the park by the average fan, the appeal of the higher-priced merchandise must in large part be directed to the other hours of the day and week. That is how the retained scorecard may come in handy.

Away-from-Fenway services and merchandise require customer effort, in which time, distance, transportation, and especially money, currently exert greater restrictive influence than in the previous several years. Rising prices and dwindling incomes put the pressure also on the advertisers, who have to adjust to new and difficult situations. The scorecards of 1975 and later may well reflect some of this.

The author has one very pertinent suggestion to the advertisers and the ladies already have guessed it. Enlarge your appeal horizons at long last, no longer focus just on him, or on him and her. Let them concentrate a bit on putting some capable, clever female merchandisers to work on attracting other women toward what they really cannot afford not to buy! If the author's analysis is worth anything in the marketplace, it clearly shows too much of an advertising focus, through tradition unhampered by progress, on the male.

After all, the girls have a fine track record as buyers! In this day of supposed equal rights and opportunity, give the women their opportunity to show their best at discovering attractive bargains, specials, new items bouncing with the times, and to show their famous enthusiasm, determination, and endurance in the sales areas. Though the cry, "Batter Up" still produces more men than women at the plate, "Buyer Up," if directed properly, well may bring out a championship team of women!

IS PITCHING
THE MOST IMPORTANT
DEPARTMENT IN BASEBALL?

Comparing and contrasting pitching and batting is somewhat like, in World War II terms, doing the same for an American aircraft carrier's defensive (such as damage control personnel, procedures, equipment) and offensive (such as attack bombers, torpedo and fighter planes) power. One cannot do without the other. In baseball there is a paradox. If pitching is more important than batting, defense is more significant than offense. But each game is officially decided by which team scores more runs.

Unlike football, basketball, and hockey, baseball guarantees much more equal opportunity. The first three sports deservedly illustrate the well-known claim, "The best defense is a good offense." Possession and control of the ball or puck is highly important. But with a few legal exceptions, baseball insures each team three outs each half inning.

Win still is the actual name of sports, baseball of course included. Close seasonal statistics differences among two or more teams is of limited value; how contending teams made out in various season's series with the other clubs, in the "must" and close games, presents more valid information. When there are considerable percentage differences among the several teams in both batting and pitching, these are fairly reliable indicators of why the teams finished in the order they did, yet no complete explanation.

Although the average fan since 1920 doubtless is more interested in batting than pitching, even he qualifies his opinion. Great pitching by the favorite team is heartily accepted, and opponents' hurling taken full advantage of by the same favorites' sturdy batters is an even greater delight. As in comparing the values of bananas and oranges, so, too, with horsehide and wood, hallowed tools of the profession, not everything can be resolved. But we do have some research findings to support the opinion of the author, and many others, that pitching is extremely important.

Examining the seasonal averages of the 1901-1974 League campaigns, in specific relation to each season's champion club, in 35 of those years (47 percent of the time) the annual winners had a better team rating in ERA than in batting. In contrast, in 22 campaigns (30 percent of the time) the winners had a better hitting than hurling record. The remaining 17 (23 percent) found the victors with identical pitching and batting placement, proof that they were strong, well-balanced clubs. Another way to express the significance of these facts is to state that ERA averages have been stronger factors than batting for pennant winners 61 percent of the time. Most timely, the 1974 Oakland champions put in the record the greatest League variation to date; first in ERA, 11th in batting.

Twelve earlier champion teams had at least a four-place difference in their ERA and team batting positions, and in 9, an obvious 75 percent, pitching exerted a greater influence on their final standing:

Table 1
UNUSUAL VARIATIONS, ERA AND BATTING

Champion Team	Year	Batting Position	ERA Position
Chicago	1901	5	1
Chicago	1906	8	2
Detroit	1908	1	6
Philadelphia	1913	1	6

Champion Team	Year	Batting Position	ERA Position
BOSTON	1918	6	2
New York	1938	6	1
St. Louis	1944	7	2
New York	1955	5	1
Chicago	1959	6	1
BOSTON	1967	1	8
Oakland	1972	6	2
Oakland	1973	6	2
Oakland	1974	11	1

Commentary: The 1967 Red Sox had only a comparative small disadvantage in ERA, which batting prowess overcame, and they won the deciding games, which Minnesota and Detroit did not. Note Oakland's wide variation in their 3 championship seasons to date; all on the side of excellent pitching.

The First Commandment of baseball is to finish first. If one is a realist, final positions are the only 100 percent factor. For years the traditional sequence of published stats in the *Official Guides* has been batting, fielding, then pitching. Although the average fan would reject the following suggestion to Mr. Spink as upsetting to batters' images and tradition, the author believes the times are overdue to rearrange the order into: pitching, batting, fielding.

Trends and patterns in the distribution of individual seasonal leaders in ERA, percentage of victories, and most wins among the several active clubs are presented in tabular form:

Table 2
LEAGUE INDIVIDUAL ERA LEADERS

Team	1901-1919	1920-1941	1942-1960	1961-1974	Total
Chicago	4	3	4	3	14
Cleveland	4	3	3	2	12
BOSTON	4	4	1	1	10
New York		4	6		10
Detroit	1	3	1		5
Oakland				3	3
Baltimore			1	1	2

Table 3
LEAGUE INDIVIDUAL PITCHING
PERCENTAGE LEADERS

Team	1901-1919	1920-1941	1942-1960	1961-1974	Total
New York	1	9	9	2	21
BOSTON	4	1	4		9
Chicago	4		3	2	9
Cleveland	2	3	2	1	8
Detroit	3	2	1	1	7
Baltimore				5	5
Oakland				2	2
Minnesota				1	1

Table 4
LEAGUE INDIVIDUAL MOST VICTORIES

Team	1901-1919	1920-1941	1942-1960	1961-1974	Total
Cleveland	1	6	8	1	16
New York	2	6	3	3	14
Detroit	1	1	7	4	13
Chicago	3	2	2	3	10
BOSTON	4	1	3	1	9
Baltimore			1	2	3
Minnesota				3	3
Oakland				1	1
Texas				1	1

Table 5
COMBINED INDIVIDUAL TOTALS, 1901-1974

Team	ERA	Percentage	Victories	Total
New York	10	21	14	45
Cleveland	12	8	16	36
Chicago	14	9	10	33
BOSTON	10	9	9	28
Detroit	5	7	13	25
Baltimore	2	5	3	10
Oakland	3	2	1	6
Minnesota		1	3	4
Texas			1	1

Table 6
**TEAM AND INDIVIDUAL ERA LEADERS,
COMBINED, 1901-1974**

Team	Individual Leaders	Team Leaders	Combined Total
New York	10	21	31
Chicago	14	13	27
Cleveland	12	11	23
BOSTON	10	5	15
Baltimore	2	10	12
Detroit	5	1	6
Oakland	3	1	4

Commentary on Tables 2-6: New York has had amazing pitching depth, as indicated by the 21 team ERA leaderships, and by coincidence an equal number of percentage leaders who obviously seldom lost games. Chicago and Cleveland, well-placed in pitching performances, were not frequent League champions because of batting problems. The Red Sox rarely showed pitching depth but frequently were aided by their hitting. The Orioles, in twenty-one years since their League readmission, have possessed outstanding hurling.

How about the Boston Red Sox's various pitching profiles in the first seventy-four years of the club's history? First, their individual League leaders in three major pitching departments:

Table 7
**RED SOX LEAGUE LEADERS, ERA,
PERCENTAGE AND VICTORIES**

Name	ERA	Percentage	Most Wins	Totals
Young	1	1	3	5
Grove	4	1		5
Wood	1	2	1	4
Hughson		1	1	2
Parnell	1		1	2
Leonard	1			1
Ruth	1			1
Jones		1		1
Ferrell			1	1
Ferriss		1		1
Kramer		1		1
Kinder		1		1
Sullivan			1	1
Lonborg			1	1
Tiant	1			1
	10	9	9	28

Table 7 Commentary: Most of the names are those either of old-timers or semi-old-timers. Only Luis Tiant is a contemporary Bostonian. Clearly there has been a general Red Sox lack of effective pitchers; only occasional ones have stood out and the club has suffered accordingly without steady, reliable, durable "numbers one and two."

The Boston top-ten career pitching percentage leaders, who have had at least 100 decisions, reveal much information, both direct and implied. The modest list of only 5 who won 100 or more games is quite small for an original League member. Each one in the table obviously had good teams behind him, or he would not be there. Some Red Sox pitchers not in this list performed well but did so in periods of weak Red Sox teams, such as in 1922-1932.

Table 8
RED SOX CAREER PITCHING LEADERS, PERCENTAGE
(100 OR MORE DECISIONS)

Name	Years	Total Years	Won	Lost	P.C.
Joe Wood	1908-1915	8	112	57	.662
Babe Ruth*	1914-1919	6	89	46	.659
Tex Hughson	1941-1949	8†	96	54	.640
Lefty Grove*	1934-1941	8	105	62	.629
Cy Young	1901-1908	8	190	113	.627
Ellis Kinder	1948-1955	8	86	52	.623
Mel Parnell*	1947-1956	10	123	75	.621
Wes Ferrell	1934-1937	4	62	40	.608
Jesse Tannehill*	1904-1908	5	60	40	.600
Joe Dobson	1941-50; 1954	9‡	106	72	.596

*indicates left-hander
†indicates one year military service
‡two years military service

In fairness, four additional pitchers must be mentioned from the group in less than 100 decisions because of their high averages. Ferriss, 65-30 .864; Shore, 56-32 .636; Foster, 58-34 .630. Of the actives, Tiant, at 58-39 .597 is on the threshold.

Commentary on Table 8: Note the slight prevalence of right-handers. For several reasons, the career longevity of outstanding Red Sox pitchers has been damagingly brief, averaging just un-

JOHN "BUCK" FREEMAN (1901-1907). Outfielder-first baseman, he was a fearsome slugger with ability, confidence, rhythm, and power. First American League player to hit two homers in a regular season contest. His 121 RBIs in 1902 remained a club record for thirty-four years. Years later, Buck was photographed with Babe Ruth, when the latter's 29 homers in 1919 eclipsed Buck's earlier team record of 13, set in 1903.

AL "KIP" SELBACH (1904-1906). In addition to his fine catch in the 1904 pennant-clincher, Kip was a practitioner of the old adage that patience is a virtue. In no hurry to swing and being quite selective of rival pitchers' offerings, he became almost a landmark at first by reason of walks and his base hits. This splendid, autographed portrait was typical of Horner's Studio in Boston.

BILL DINNEEN (1902-1907). Earlier he had aroused Collins's ire (recorded in Lewis's diary) for not joining the team in 1901. Overall 87-85, in his first three years scored 65 wins. 3-1 in 1903 Series, the next season he showed perfect durability, never having to be removed from a game he started. 1905 no-hitter against Chicago. Later served as a League umpire and is so honored at Cooperstown.

FRED PARENT (1901-1907). A small, wiry, agile player, Fred was team's original shortstop and proved remarkably durable both during playing years and in later life, attaining an age of 96. Twice over .300 and a fine fielder, Fred later was a frequent guest of honor at Fenway for annual State of Maine day. In 1953, recollecting Cy Young's 1904 perfect game, the still ebullient Parent wrote, "The game of all time for me. What a game!"

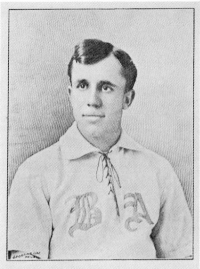

FREDERICK PARENT
SHORTSTOP OF THE BOSTON (A. L.) CLUB OF 1902

Fred. Parent.

JESSE TANNEHILL

Jesse Mills Tannehill

JESSE TANNEHILL (1904-1908). He brought with him a fine major league background record of 131-72. Immediately this southpaw gave necessary balance to Boston's otherwise right-handed staff of Young, Dinneen, Gibson, and Winter. In 1904 Jesse no-hitted Chicago, a year later had most team wins, with 21. Overall 60-40 for Boston, Tannehill in retirement correspondence paid sincere tribute to a pitcher's best friend; teammates' good fielding, including always a particular favorite, the double play.

BOSTON RECORD	
Year	B.A.
1901	310
1902	318
1903	279
1904	300
1905	258
1906	286

CHARLES STAHL
RED SOX RECORD HOLDER
Triples(tie) 22 1903
LEAGUE LEADER

CHARLES "CHICK" STAHL (1901-1906). Elder brother of Jake, in 1904 he made a club record for triples, 22, later tied by Speaker. In the 1903 Series, Chick hit three of his specialty, when the team made an unbeatable record of 16 because then accepted ground rules allowed three bases on each fairly batted ball into the outfield standing crowds. His tragic, untimely death occurred on March 28, 1907, during spring training, when he was Manager-player.

RED SOX STARS

FRANK ARELLANES
BOSTON AMERICAN
PITCHER
THROWING TO CATCH
A MAN OFF THIRD

SUPPLEMENTS
TO
BOSTON SUNDAY POST

FRANK ARELLANES (1908-1910). Frank's brief major league activity (24-22) was entirely with Boston. 1909 was his best season; 17 wins, most team innings pitched. He also was active off the mound and joined his teammates in wise defensive maneuvers. When in New York, after uniforming in their hotel, they would proceed by taxi to the Highlanders' park, with blinds carefully drawn, to avoid fan pelting with fruits and vegetables. In this period, loyalties ran high, food costs low.

BOSTON BASEBALL IN THE GRAND MANNER! An official, formal engraved invitation, in color, to the 1907 Opener. But the season proved quite undistinguished in Boston, though club managed to climb one notch out of the cellar. Of more lasting significance was team president John I. Taylor's wise decision of adopting Red Sox as team's nickname, more discernible in later years on at-home shirts than in dwindling amount of red in their stockings. Mr. Taylor also acted as his own scout, persuading such players as Hooper, Lewis, Arellanes, and Janvrin to sign.

The Boston American League
Base Ball Club
requests the honor of your presence at
The Opening Game of the Season
Tuesday afternoon April 16th 1907
at three o'clock
Huntington Avenue Ball Grounds
Boston

EDDIE CICOTTE (1908-1912). As things turned out, his later career was filled with mixed emotions, frequently sad; earlier, with Boston, he was under pressure for not doing as well as expected. 49-45 for the Red Sox, he just missed out being on the 1912 Champions, being traded that spring to the White Sox. 1909-1910 were his best Boston years. Eddie, together with teammates Carrigan and Lord, gained inclusion in the 25-player card set of the Philadelphia Caramel Company, of which this is a fine example.

HARRY LORD (1907-1910). From Bates College, he played third and captained the 1909 Bostons, whom he also led in batting, with .311. 1909 was a turning point; team rose to third, highest rung since 1904. One reason was great speed of the club; four regulars stole a total of 124 bases, with Harry the leader at 36. Home-game support related to this; 668,965 paid, not to be topped until Fenway Park's 29th season, 1940, despite four championship teams at the new ball grounds before that year.

HARRY NILES (1908-1910). A versatile utility player, he not only was used in the infield but in 1909 was the team's left fielder. This striking card was typical of the period, when such leading cigarette companies as Fez, Old Mill, and Turkey Red issued color series of baseball cards which have retained their artistic appeal for over sixty-five years.

A CHANGE IN SCENERY BRINGS IMMEDIATE SUCCESS! Fenway Park opened in April, 1912; this view shows first base grandstand seats and the right field pavilion. There appeared to be both a physical and spiritual connection between the old and new parks. So good was the Huntington Avenue Grounds' turf that the Red Sox brought it with them to Jersey Street. The 1912 Bostons then proceeded in both senses to follow in the footsteps of their distinguished 1903 and 1904 predecessors.

THOMAS "BUCK" O'BRIEN (1911-1913). Brockton-born "Buck's" brief Boston career was noteworthy beyond a 28-21 record because he was winning pitcher in the first game played at the then new Fenway Park in 1912. His 19 wins that season aided Red Sox pennant drive, though in subsequent Series he was 0-2. Many years later he recalled of the championship campaign, "When I would get behind, which I frequently did in the early innings of a number of games, my infielders would gather around and tell me not to allow any more runs, while they promised on their part to get them all back, and more. That's just what happened several times."

69

CHARLES "SEA LION" HALL (1909-1913). According to teammate Hooper, Charlie obtained this unusual nickname "because he could imitate the bark or call of the sea lion." Lifetime 43-33, Hall was particularly effective in even years. In the 1912 Series at the bat he went three for four to establish a still-standing best average for a moundsman.

"ROUGH" BILL CARRIGAN (1906-1916). From the College of the Holy Cross and a down-Easter from Lewiston, Maine, he served ten distinguished years behind the plate, also seven as manager (1913-1916, again, 1927-1929). The derivation of his nickname in part was because Bill stood his defensive ground at home with resolution against flying spikes of such would-be scorers as Ty Cobb. Members of his two championship teams extolled him, then and later, as a wise, alert, forceful leader who brought the best out of his players, individually and collectively.

AWAY-FROM-THE-PARK FRINGE BENEFITS. Fifth-place 1911 Red Sox formed a singing quartet, of pitchers McHale and O'Brien, utilityman Bradley, and professional singer Lyons. Appearing on Keith's famous winter circuit, 1911-1913, they acquired additional box office advantage of becoming World Champions the middle year. Hugh Bradley's claim to fame was hitting first Fenway Park homer, in 1912, over the original wooden left field fence, considerably lower than the "green monster" of more recent times.

1912 SERIES AS TIGHT AS CLOTHESPINS ON COVER SOX! Interesting interior Boston program material, beside baseball, included availability of Stutz roadsters at $2,000 and Arrow shirts at $1.50. So program confident were the Bostons that the stage was challenged. In particular, both actor George Arliss and the production Disraeli in which he would appear the next week, were told in no uncertain type, "They've got to go some to beat our Red Sox."

71

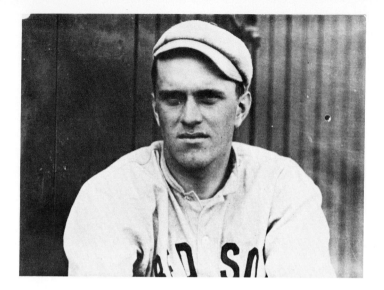

I think beating Matty in the Series and holding them to two runs in eighteen innings were outstanding in my memory.

Would like a print of the club if you have time, thanks

Hugh Bedient

HUGH BEDIENT (1912-1914). En route to overall 43-35, Hugh was a very significant influence in Red Sox 1912 triumphs. 18-9 for regular season as a rookie, in Series had a remarkable 0.50 ERA, yielding only 10 hits in the mentioned 18 innings. Three times he opposed Mathewson, and the Boston youngster outpitched the great Christy, then completing his 12th distinguished season. Note last sentence of letter; many ball players do not retain team pictures, even those of great accomplishment.

Joe Wood

BOSTON RECORD
WON 115 LOST 56

"SMOKY" JOE WOOD (1908-1915). His nickname a tribute to his blinding speed, Joe still holds 4 Boston pitching records, shares a fifth. Had a 1911 no-hitter against St. Louis, generally his "cousins." 1912 was his year; won 34, including 16 straight, won 3 more in Series. Bad arm cut short his brilliant mound career, but his 112-57 still is the Boston career best percentage. He wrote the author in 1953, "I have always had one regret: Just at the peak of my career my arm went bad. With the wonderful Red Sox team I may have been lucky and set some real records."

about the dinner although I recall names of most of the players. The names of Brady, Kelley, Higgins, McMahon do not come to me at all.

"Puts" as we all called Putnam's was next door to the conservatory of music and only 2 or 3 blocks from the Old Huntington Ave. Park. We walked to and from the park.

The big moment for me in World Series play was in 1st game 1912 against Giants, at Polo Grounds. As I remember we were leading by one run, last of 9th, one out. Giants on 2nd and 3rd. An error or sacrifice fly would tie the score and a hit would beat us. For the second out I struck out Art Fletcher and then McGraw sent in Doc Crandall, who had never struck out at the Polo Grounds. His strike out was the final out. We rec'd lapel button, with diamond in 1912 but I

WOOD'S HAPPIER RECOLLECTION. He described his greatest Boston thrill as staving off a desperate New York rally, first game of 1912 Series, bottom of the ninth, Giants on second and third, only one out, and Boston clinging to a 4-3 lead.

73

CALL OUT THE RESERVES! The Royal Rooters, before seventh 1912 Series game at Fenway, on arrival at park were angered to find expected reserved seats had been sold to others. Consequently, organization swarmed on field, complete with band, and indignation, and refused to leave. Game was delayed some twenty-five minutes while officers afoot, bolstered by reinforcements and led by mounted police from nearby Station Sixteen, cleared grounds to permit play. Whereupon Giants romped to 11-4 win, evening Series at three each.

Canton Mass
July 7, 1959

Mr Clark Jr,
Dear Sir,—
          In reply to your
letter about my biggest
Thrill.
Well I think it was in
The 1912 World Series
when I made the 2 base hit
in the 7th inning That
Tided the score – 2 – 2
and we went on to win
in the 10th inning.
I am sorry I havent got a
picture in uniform as the
reporters have been taken
Them as years go by
                    Yours Truly,
                    Olaf Henriksen

OLAF HENRIKSEN (1911-1917). Danish-born, he hit 13 doubles for Boston, but the one that counted most was number six. This valuable utility outfielder smashed a pinch-hit double off third base which scored Stahl with tie run in 7th inning of 1912 Series finale. Olaf, on three World Champions, was used only sparingly, averaging about 44 games per season. His happiest memory, of course, was the big hit.

Harry Hooper unquestionably saved the game and the series for Boston in the sixth inning with one of the greatest of all World Series catches, a play depriving Doyle of a home run and preventing the Giants from winning in nine innings. Larry hit a terrific line drive to the temporary bleacher in deep right center, and it looked like curtains. Hooper ran back as far as he could, and threw himself backward over a low railing, and half-supported by the backs of the crowd, reached upward and caught the ball just as it was about to fall into the stand. It was a magnificent effort, though the Giants claimed it wasn't a legal catch. John B. Foster, former editor of Spalding's *Guide* and later secretary of the Giants, insisted to his dying day that Hooper was entirely off the playing field when the ball was caught and that Doyle's home run should have been allowed. But Boston fans never bothered about such a technicality, and that catch made Harry a hero as long as he remained in Boston. ✱

SAVED THE GAME! Considered to this day at least one of the World Series' greatest catches, and undoubtedly from a Boston point of view the greatest, Harry Hooper later provided a minute and thrilling description of his sixth-inning out against Larry Doyle which defensively kept the Red Sox alive in the final 1912 Series contest. Note Harry's statement about his concentration on the ball, "It seemed to be suspended in the air." Hooper caught it, bare-handed.

✱From Boston Red Sox by F. Lieb. © 1947 by F. Lieb. Used by permission of G. P. Putnam's Sons, New York.

FIRST ROW

CLARKE, WOOD, BEDIENT, HOOPER, YERKES, STAHL

SECOND ROW

HENRIKSEN, WAGNER, CADY, O'BRIEN, WHEELER

COLLINS, LEWIS

CARRIGAN

CADY, COLLINS, HALL, WHEELER

1912 WORLD CHAMPIONS. The Sporting News, founded in 1886, and famed St. Louis weekly and "baseball Bible," published this special pictorial. Actually, on the day team picture was published, the Series was even, one game each, plus a tie game. It was a great Boston year, from start to finish of the glorious spectrum. Team made an all-time Red Sox record of 105 wins, only 47 defeats. Financially, in terms of the times, the players also did very well; each winning Series share amounting to $4,024.

77

STAHL Boston Amer.

GARLAND "JAKE" STAHL (1903; 1908-1913). Chick's younger brother and a University of Illinois man, he was team's first baseman in 1910, also League leader in homers. Appointed manager in early 1912, he hit .301 and led club to both titles. Fast afoot, he was a frequent base stealer. This card was number 38 in a combination baseball-boxing series.

TRIS SPEAKER (1907-1915). Boston's greatest center fielder, Tris eight times took League fielding honors (putouts 4, assists 2, double plays 2) and four times with bat (doubles 2, hits and total bases one each). Red Sox's leading hitter for six straight seasons, his career mark was .336, second only to Ted Williams. In 1912 he won the Chalmers Award as League's MVP; a four-door Chalmers touring car, valued at $1950. Speaker still holds club record for seasonal hits (222) and triples (tie, at 22) and in 1969 was chosen on the Greatest Red Sox Team Ever.

SPEAKER Boston Amer.

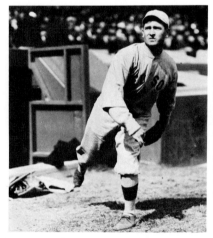

GEORGE "RUBE" FOSTER (1913-1917). A very strong pitcher until suffering arm injury, nevertheless he was 58-34 lifetime. 1915 was his year, without question. In regular season his record was 19-8, also the team leader in wins and innings pitched. During the World Series, he won both his starts, also made a record at the bat. Going four for eight, Foster created a hit total for a hurler not exceeded, nor likely to be, by any Series pitcher since. In 1916 "Rube" no-hitted New York.

78

YERKES-BOSTON-AMER.

STEVE YERKES (1909-1914). He played second in championship season, batted in decisive runs in 1912 Series first game, scored winner in final. 1913 Spalding's Official Base Ball Guide stated, "The New York outfielder [Devore] caught the ball and made a game effort to stop the flying Yerkes at the plate, but failed to do so." Sixty-two years later Harry Hooper recalled, "The joy and jubilation we experienced at winning after it looked as if we were going to lose cannot be expressed in words." Each victorious Boston received as a World Champion Emblem a gold lapel button, with inset diamond.

THE INCOMPARABLE OUTFIELD. From a Boston point of view not only best in 1911-1915, but all-time greatest. They did everything well. Collectively they stole 396 bases, afield recorded many assists and double plays. Of all the fly balls snagged by them, Speaker in center grabbed 41 percent, Lewis in left 30 percent, and Hooper in right 27 percent. At bat, in 1911 each was comfortably over .300. In their two World Series, trio averaged .290. For their Boston service, one of the three, generally Speaker, led team in 14 of possible 15 of the three major batting departments.

RAY COLLINS (1909-1915). Signed directly after graduation from the University of Vermont, Ray's ultimate record was 89-62. His three best seasons were 1912-1914. In 1912 Series he did not issue a walk in 14 1/3 innings. Third Boston to win 20 in successive campaigns, sturdy Collins on September 22, 1914, became first Red Sox to win two complete games in one day. He twice was team leader in wins, once each in ERA and innings pitched.

Ray W. Collins

CHARLES "HEINIE" WAGNER (1906-1918). Durable "Heinie" had eleven years with the club, six as regular shortstop, two at second. Although his career bat mark was around .250, Wagner achieved an almost 40 percent additional arrival on base by walks. A captain of the team and thrice a World Champion, he returned in 1930 as manager. This fine photograph was supplied by a special supplement to the Boston Sunday Herald in 1909.

80

der eight years. Wood hurt his arm at the peak of his achievements, and turned to outfielding. Ruth was a happy and willing victim of his batting prowess. Four of the group were veterans of many seasons with other clubs before they came to Boston; Young, 11; Grove, 9; Tannehill, 8; and Ferrell, 7. Wood, Ruth, Hughson, and Parnell began their major league careers with the Red Sox. Only Wood and Ruth (but 1-2) appeared from the great period, 1912-1918.

Obviously, individual pitching tables, or two or three combined, cannot possibly provide a reasonable in-depth profile of the best qualified all-around career hurlers. The following compilation is an admitted hybrid, combining Red Sox who led the League in 5 seasonal categories and their position in 9 intra-Boston career departments. As a compromise it establishes the following, in order of merit:

Table 9
BEST RED SOX ALL-AROUND PITCHERS

Red Sox Career Pitching Leaders	League Season Leader					Red Sox Career Position								
	ERA	%	Wins	K	Saves	%	Wins	G	GS	CG	Inn.	Shut Outs	K	Saves
Young	1	1	3	1		4	1	2	1	1	1	1	1	
Wood	1	2	1			1	3			4	10	2	2	
Parnell	1		1			7	2	5	2	6	2	4	10	
Grove	4	1				5	5	7	5	6			8	
Hughson		1	1	1		3	6				8			
Kinder		1			1	6		1						2
Leonard	1				1		10		9			3	7	
Monbouquette							6		3		3	9	3	
Sullivan			1				9	10	4		8		4	
Ruth	1					2	10			7		7		
Dobson							10	4	8	6	10	5	7	
Lonborg		1		1									6	
Fornieles					1			3						4
Radatz				2			6							1
Winter								9	3	4				
Dinneen								9	2	9	9			
Brewer							8	5		7			9	

Commentary on Table 9: The incomparable Young is unassailable in his top position and leadership over all the others. Of course he was not a relief pitcher and could not score in that area. Wood and Parnell easily were superior to their challengers. The value of Leonard, Monbouquette, and Sullivan, perhaps not realized by many, is apparent. In general, the player sequence is very close to that of the career top ten. This broader table, as is true of leading Red Sox batters, shows the breadth of versatility of these highly competent athletes.

Shifting attention to no-hitters, where the Red Sox based on the actual stats of 1901-1974 achieved success on the average of .00123 percent of the time in terms of games played, the club has done well in these unpredictable accomplishments. As records prove, these have been achieved not only by great pitchers, such as Young and Wood, but by average and even under-average ones, in terms of pitcher appraisals. Any starter—and Shore was an exception—has a chance if he and his teammates can put it all together, regardless of his recent performances.

Contrary to American folk-belief, no lasting damage was done by no-hitters to later career performances of Red Sox pitchers. Two-thirds (8 of 12) of this distinguished group did not appear earlier in table 8 for various reasons. Monbouquette and Dinneen did not have high enough percentages; Foster, Leonard, and Shore lacked 100 decisions; and Ehmke was with some of the worst teams in Boston history, and was joined later in losing career records by both Wilson and Morehead.

On the more cheerful side, Young and Leonard were repeaters, while nine of the dozen were right-handers (Boston would have been equally happy if the ratio had favored lefties). Ten, by unscheduled thoughtfulness, were fashioned in Boston. Finally, the spread between Ehmke's no-hitter (with a last-place Red Sox team) and Parnell's was over thirty-three years, the longest drought in Boston baseball history.

Table 10
RED SOX NO-HITTERS

Date	Pitcher	Opponent	Score
May 5, 1904*	Cy Young	Phil	3-0†
Aug 17, 1904*	Jesse Tannehill (L)	Chi	6-0
Sept 27, 1905*	Bill Dinneen	Chi	2-0
June 30, 1908	Cy Young	N Y	8-0
July 29, 1911*	Joe Wood	St L	5-0
June 21, 1916*	George Foster	N Y	2-0
Aug 30, 1916*	Hub Leonard (L)	St L	4-0
June 23, 1917*	Ernie Shore	Wash	4-0‡
June 3, 1918	Hub Leonard (L)	Detr	5-0
Sept 7, 1923	Howard Ehmke	Phil	4-0
July 14, 1956*	Mel Parnell (L)	Chi	4-0
June 26, 1962*	Earl Wilson	L A	2-0
Aug 1, 1962	Bill Monbouquette	Chi	1-0
Sept 16, 1965*	Dave Morehead	Clev	4-0

*indicates home game
†perfect game, 27 batters
‡perfect game, 26 batters
(L) Lefty

One criticism to which Red Sox managers such as Joe Cronin and Darrell Johnson have been subject to from second-guessers, not unfairly, has been their tendency on a number of occasions to linger too long with a faltering starting pitcher. This author is hard-nosed and is of the school that believes a tottering hurler will get worse rather than better. Upsetting as it may be to a pitcher, win is the name of the game. The ready availability of numerous relievers adds credence to the concept, "Bring in a fresh arm in case of doubt." Table 10 contains the Utopia! It is quite possible manager Darrell Johnson will skillfully blend the considerable talents of the Red Sox to make them a team to remember. May their moundsmen be inspired by the occasional pitching glories of the past, among their several incentives to win.

BATTING SIGNIFICANCE: BOSTON'S PROFILE IN THE ATTACK

Most people, in sports where there is a choice, much prefer the attack to defense, although the administrative and player personnel know there is a necessary balance between the two, and one cannot be neglected to the disadvantage of the other, or especially to the team's total effort. As one might expect, the old-time ball players had the early opportunity to make philosophic observations about the sport, especially as to the secret of a successful batting performance.

One of these was Willie Keeler, famous National Leaguer from 1892-1910, .300 hitter for thirteen consecutive seasons and elected to the Hall of Fame in 1939. He practiced what he preached, which was: "Hit 'em where they ain't!" These words have stood the test of time. However, up until 1920 the skills of all-around batting versatility had to be practical and applied, especially since the dead ball prevented many home runs from being powered. Thus, for many years the individual big league batting champion was held in highest esteem until the 1920s when the lively ball successfully encouraged fandom to honor the reigning home run champions far more than the batting percentage leaders.

Old official baseball guides pictorially reflected the dominance of the batting champions; the only individuals to be given full-page pictures were the two bat winners of the previous campaign. Man for man, both spectators and players (even including a few philosophic opposing pitchers) had the highest admiration for the few batters who consistently would get on base by using the various sanctioned means, such as singles, including leg hits, extra base hits, well-earned walks, getting hit by pitched balls, and, of course, taking quick and full base-path advantage of fielding errors of commission or omission. The art of batting chiefly consisted of taking a good cut at the ball, yet in intent controlled sufficiently, with applied skill and some good fortune, to hit it safely rather than far. Over the years the all-time best League batters have included both the skilled and the power hitters, sometimes those with both qualifications.

Great hitters are admitted as a breed to have many mutual talents; ability, dedication, concentration, versatility, aggressiveness, and endurance. They have been students of the game, gaining their doctorate equivalents both at the plate and in shrewd observation of the opposition from the on-deck area or on the bench, awaiting their turn at bat. Twelve selected batting categories are chosen as the basis for determining the broad profiles of the Red Sox hitters over the years, so that a reasonably representative comparison can be made, and the value of certain players established within this framework.

Table 11
COMPARATIVE STATS, INTRA-RED SOX
CAREER LEADING BATTERS

Intra-Red Sox Career Leading Batters	Games	Batt. Aver.	RBI	At Bats	Hits	2B	3B	HR	Runs	TB	EBH	Slug. Aver.
1. Williams*	1	1	1	2	1	1	7	1	1	1	1	1
2. Yastrzemski*	2		3	1	2	2		2	2	2	2	8
3. Doerr	3		2	3	3	3	4	3	3	3	3	
4. Hooper*	4			4	4	8	1		5	5	8	
5. DiMaggio	5	9	10	5	5	4			4	4	4	
6. Foxx		3	4					4	7	8	5	2
7. Speaker*		2			8	9	2		8	9	9	7
8. Malzone	6		7	6	6	10		9		6	10	
9. Petrocelli	7		8	7				5		7	6	
10. Cronin	10	8	5						10	10	7	6
11. Goodman*	9	6		8	7	7			9			
12. Lewis	8		9	9	10	6	10					

*Left-handed batter

What may one conclude? Williams comfortably was the most outstanding, then Yaz and Doerr closely matched for 2-3, Hooper and Dom DiMaggio in a tie for 4th, Foxx 6th, and Speaker 7th; with Malzone, Petrocelli, and Cronin almost in a triple tie, then Goodman and Duffy Lewis. Most of these players were from the third period (1942-1960), with three from the first and two still active. The speed of a number of early Red Sox, conducive to high position in career Boston triples, is worth mention even today. Closely bunched, old-time heroes Buck Freeman, Larry Gardner, Hobe Ferris, Jimmy Collins, Lewis, and Fred Parent still stand 3-5-6-8-9-9 (tie) in that list, behind Harry Hooper and Tris Speaker. Only Bob Doerr (4) and Williams (7) have been able to crack this otherwise "old-timers'" special preserve.

League Individual Batting Champions. Sixty-four percent of these, through 1974, were left-handed, having enjoyed the obvious stride's advantage over righties in close plays at first. In 1901-1919, the Red Sox did not gain a title, in a period dominated by Cobb, who was the perennial leader, 1907-1919, with the exception only of 1916. During 1920-1941 the Tigers's Heilmann won four times, but the Red Sox in their thirty-second year produced their first leader, Dale Alexander, and in 1941 Ted Williams at .406—a Boston record and probably the last member of the ".400 club." During 1942-1960, Boston won 7 times; Williams (5), Goodman and Runnels, one each. In the most recent period, Yastrzemski (3) and Runnels for a second time brought crowns to Fenway.

Table 12

INDIVIDUAL BATTING CHAMPIONS, BY CLUBS

Team	1901-1919	1920-1941	1942-1960	1961-1974	Total
Detroit	12	6	3	1	22
BOSTON		3	7	4	14
Cleveland	4	1	2		7
Minnesota				7	7
New York		4	2		6
Chicago		1	1		2
Baltimore				1	1
California				1	1

As in other baseball averages, of which only the final standings are definitive, team performance in relation to the other clubs is of much greater value than that of selected individuals. Under the early leadership of Cobb, later of Heilmann, Detroit holds a comfortable numerical lead in team batting over the Red Sox, well-placed as usual, in second. The Yankees are just behind Boston, while in the most recent time period, Minnesota (with particular assists from Carew and Oliva) is on the way to a new record, if maintained, of percent of leaderships.

Table 13
AMERICAN LEAGUE TEAM BATTING LEADERS

Team	1901-1919	1920-1941	1942-1960	1961-1974	Total
Detroit	6	7	2	1	16
BOSTON	1	4	5	2	12
New York		4	6	1	11
Cleveland	4	2	2		8
Minnesota				6	6
Chicago	1		4		5
Baltimore	1			2	3
Oakland				1	1
Kansas City				1	1

Once again, all-around League batting performance, as earlier cited relative to an intra-Red Sox comparison, provides much more depth perception than just one statistical table. Thus, the profile of Red Sox American League leaders in some 11 selected batting categories provides some interesting, significant results for the club's history to date:

Table 1
RED SOX LEAGUE BATTING LEADERS, 11 CATEGORIES
LISTED BY FREQUENCY OF TITLE

Red.Sox League Batting Leaders	Batt. Ave.	RBI	TB	Slug. %	Hits	2B	3B	HR	BB	Runs	S.B.
Williams	6	4	6	9		2		4	8	6	
Yastrzemski	3	1	2	3	2	3		1	2	3	
Foxx	1	1	1	2				1	1		
Ruth		1	1	2				2		1	

Red Sox League Batting Leaders	Batt. Ave.	RBI	TB	Slug. %	Hits	2B	3B	HR	BB	Runs	S.B.
Freeman		2	1					1	1		
Jensen		3						1			1
Speaker			1		2	2					
DiMaggio								1		2	1
Smith			1			2					
Pesky					3						
Doerr				1			1				
Dougherty					1					1	
Werber											2
Stephens		2									
Runnels	2										
Stuart		1	1								
Team's Total League Leaderships	14	15*	15	17	9	12	4†	11	11	13	7

*Williams, Stephens tied in 1949; Williams, Dropo in 1950.
†Freeman, J. Stahl tied in 1904; also Doerr and DiMaggio, 1950, and Fisk, 1972.

Commentary on Table 14: Once again, Williams and Yaz are outstanding, as in the intra-Red Sox comparisons. Foxx is well-placed, but DiMaggio is down a little. In contrast, Ruth, Freeman, and Jensen are better positioned. Jensen had an unusual combination of League firsts; RBI and stolen bases. Williams, in extra base hits, never led in triples, indicative of modest speed. Note the general well-distributed Boston batting leaderships, with good balance except in triples and stolen bases. Unfortunately for the Red Sox, only Yaz of the group currently still is active.

Although somewhat redundant, an examination of the actual individual percentages of the Red Sox top-ten all-time batters is revealing for a number of reasons and indicates the skills of such hitters as Speaker and Jimmy Collins in the dead-ball era, sufficient to place them second and tenth, overall:

Table 15
RED SOX CAREER TOP TEN BATTERS

	Active Boston Years	Boston Career Percentage
Ted Williams*	1939-1960†	.344
Tris Speaker*	1907-1915	.336
Jimmie Foxx	1936-1942	.320
Pete Runnels*	1958-1962	.320
Johnny Pesky*	1942-1952‡	.313
Bill Goodman*	1947-1957	.306
Doc Cramer*	1936-1940	.302
Joe Cronin	1935-1945	.300
Dom DiMaggio	1940-1953‡	.298
Jimmy Collins	1901-1907	.296

*Left-handed batter
†Two complete seasons missed, only a total of 43 games played in another two because of military service
‡Three years of military service

Commentary on Table 15: Obviously, none of the above still is active. Left-handers prevailed in numbers, 6-4, also in 1-2-4-5-6-7 placement. In baseball periods, with the exception of the 20-season gap between Speaker's departure for Cleveland and Cronin's arrival from Washington, there has been a good chronological balance between the best Red Sox hitters. Also significant is the Williams footnote; what he did for his country also lopped off four playing seasons.

Conclusions on Red Sox Batting

1. It will not be easy for a present or future Red Sox batter to gain entry into the first ten. With increasing numbers of night games, probably more expansion teams and greater distances between League cities, continued loss of player-rest during night flights, three-hour time differences between the two coasts, and other factors will work against aspirants to the ".300 club." At quick thought, Jimmy Collins's .296 might appear vulnerable, but there is recent, contrary evidence. For example, in seasons 1965-1974, an obvious ten-year span, the American League has averaged only just over 5 batters per year at .300 or higher. 1968

was low, with just one (Yaz) while 1974 has been high, at 9, with Yaz again in attendance. The names, as expected, vary from year to year, another indicator of the present and implied future difficulties of reaching and maintaining a .300 status. Yaz, the second-best Red Sox career all-around batter, is at .292 in this category.

2. A counter-trend thought, to those who like pendulum theories. For the identification of the next Boston League bat champion, expect one whose surname will begin with one of the early letters in the alphabet. Note the swinging past pattern; Alexander and Foxx, then to Williams four times; to Goodman and then back to Williams twice, to Runnels twice, and Yaz three times. An early-in-the-alphabet Boston hitter is due, perhaps overdue. Burleson, Carbo, or Evans? Would Lynn and Rice agree?

3. The potential sustained good hitter, Red Sox or otherwise, will have to conquer temporary adversity, such as slumps. Study of his batting form and timing by others' observation and use of film; a broad, overdue smile from Ms. Luck, and best of all, the break-through successful application of Mr. Keeler's immortal "Hit 'em where they ain't!" will all apply to the present and future.

THE HOME RUN:
FAVORITE OF
THE BASEBALL PUBLIC

In the sporting literature of the American people, on occasion some imaginative, emotional events have been recorded, based on realistic concepts and well within the range of actuality. Ernest Lawrence Thayer was one of these contributors. In his poem, "Casey at the Bat," first published in a San Francisco newspaper on June 3, 1888, Mr. Thayer, on behalf of baseball, developed an engaging plot situation. His solution found the forces of good (home team batters) done in by the forces of evil (visitor's pitching) in a climactic bottom-of-the-ninth situation. Casey, the legendary and expected dependable long-ball striker, stranded the tying and winning runs on base as he fanned for the final out. The overconfident hero took the first two strikes, then went down, swinging. In the poem the failed hero's name frequently was mentioned, that of the villainous opposing hurler not even once. Distance hitters, rather than effective pitchers, draw more fans to the park, at Mudville or elsewhere. Home runs are first in the hit parade, according to general fan opinion.

In the American League's first nineteen years, the home run was a small factor, because of the related influences of small production and meager fan interest, in marked contrast with later seasons. In 1901-1919 the Red Sox won 7 team titles in homers, four of them consecutively, 1909-1912. Individually, they had four champions; Buck Freeman, 1903 (13), Jake Stahl, 1910 (10), and Babe Ruth twice—a tie in 1918 (11) and a new League mark in 1919 (29).

These early years well earned their later tag name of the dead-ball era, especially after the lively ball first appeared in season 1920. Boston's great outfielder, Harry Hooper, a veteran of both ages, explained the significance to the author in 1974 correspondence:

> Before 1920 after a ball was pitched three or four times it would be black. After 1919 you always could get a new white ball to hit and not one that had been batted until it was dead. . . . In the winter of 1919 the American League agreed to use a lively ball. The first one was a real rabbit and they had to slow it down a little. . . . But the League also ruled that pitchers no longer could apply foreign substances, and no more spitballers would be permitted with the exception of those at that time being recognized as regular spitball pitchers [such as Jack Quinn]. . . . Babe Ruth changed the game from one of science to one of long balls and home runs. . . . Ruth and the lively ball made the greatest change in the game's history.

The 1920 timing, whether coincidental or not, of the lively ball's appearance was good for professional baseball. Babe Ruth, the emerging most fascinating and crowd-appealing figure in ball, had just been sold by the Red Sox to the Yankees. Moreover, 8 of the 1919 League Champion Chicago White Sox had been charged with conspiring with well-known gamblers to throw the World Series of that year to Cincinnati. Subsequently, Commissioner Judge Landis barred them for life. The sport's image quickly revived and the Roaring Twenties proved highly appreciative of Ruth and the improved ball.

During 1920-1941, in sharp contrast to the continued thrills and pleasures of Yankee fans, Boston suffered through the baseball-depressed years 1922-1932, until the rising influence of then young Tom Yawkey became noticeable. Jimmie Foxx was the individual leader in 1939 (35), and Ted Williams in 1941 (37). Though not the leader in 1938, Foxx stroked a still-standing Boston seasonal mark of 50. During 1942-1960, despite his long war-period absences, Ted Williams gathered 3 more titles while the club's homer production placed it in the first 4 of that department exactly 64 percent of the time.

Thus far in the contemporary period of 1961-1974, only Tony Conigliaro, 1965 (32), and Yastrzemski, 1967 (44, a tie), have been champions, but as a homer team Boston has finished in the first three some 71 percent of the seasons, clearly an impressive and automatic run-production record, yet not supported by sufficient defensive (pitching) strength, to produce more than a single pennant.

In the following table, League seasonal home run leader totals for the various periods are shown. New York, sparked by Ruth's 10 titles (one shared with Gehrig), is an obvious clear leader, with ubiquitous Boston a good second. Note the recent Twins's and White Sox's long-ball hitting by individuals (not true of Chicago as a team), and the Indians's bunching in the third period:

Table 16
SEASONAL INDIVIDUAL HOME RUN CHAMPIONS

Team	1901-1919	1920-1941	1942-1960	1961-1974	Total
New York	2	14	6	1	23
BOSTON	4	2	3	2	11
Detroit	3	3	2		8
Cleveland			5		5
Minnesota				5	5
Chicago				3	3
Baltimore				1	1
Oakland				1	1

Comment on following Table 17: Of the 9 batters represented in the at-least-35 annual Red Sox homer production, Foxx (5), Williams (5), and Yaz have dominated. In only three years have two Boston players been in this top rating: 1949 (Williams and Stephens; 82); 1969 (Yastrzemski and Petrocelli; 80); and 1970 (Yastrzemski and Tony Conigliaro; 76).

Table 17
RED SOX TEAM SEASONAL HOME RUN LEADERS
(35 OR MORE)

Name	Number	Year
Foxx	50	1938
Yastrzemski	44	1967
Williams	43	1949
Stuart	42	1963
Foxx	41	1936
Yastrzemski	40	1970
Yastrzemski	40	1969
Petrocelli	40	1969
Stephens	39	1949
Williams	38	1957
Williams	38	1946
Williams	37	1941
T. Conigliaro	36	1970
Williams	36	1942
Foxx	36	1940
Foxx	36	1937
Harrelson	35	1968
Jensen	35	1958
Foxx	35	1939

League team rather than individual leadership in various departments, of course, is more revealing, because depth or lack of it is demonstrated. For home runs, New York, as expected, is away out front, with consecutive awesome streaks of 12 (1936-1947) and 9 (1923-1931). Symptomatic of the Yankees's great depth has been the career total of 2,413 home runs by their big five; Ruth, Mantle, Gehrig, DiMaggio, and Berra. They averaged 482 per man!

Table 18
TEAM LEADERSHIP IN HOME RUNS

Team	1901-1919	1920-1941	1942-1960	1961-1974	Total
New York	4	18	11	1	34
BOSTON	7		1	4	12
Cleveland			7	1	8
Detroit				4	4
Minnesota				2	2
Kansas City			1		1
Oakland				1	1
Chicago				1	1

Commentary on Table 18: The White Sox prove the value of perseverence; if you don't succeed the first 73 times, try once more. They did, and won their only team home run title in 1974. The Red Sox have been strong at both ends of the period. The Tigers have shown depth only in recent seasons.

For the confirmed homer buff, two additional tables are provided:

Table 19
MOST SEASONAL HOME RUNS, BY TEAMS

Team	Number	Record Year
New York	240	1961
Minnesota	225	1963
Detroit	209	1962
BOSTON	203	1970
Cleveland	183	1970
Baltimore	179	1970
Oakland	171	1970
Kansas City	166	1957; 1964
Milwaukee	145	1973
Chicago	138	1961; 1971
California	96	1971
Texas	110	1973

Table 20
LEADING ACTIVE TEAMS
(AT LEAST 10 LEAGUE SEASONS)
IN TOTAL HOME RUNS

Team	Number	Years in League	Annual Average
New York	7997	72	111
Detroit	6354	74	85
Cleveland	6156	74	83
BOSTON	6126	74	82
Chicago	4270	74	57
Baltimore	2712	23	117
Minnesota	2084	14	148
Kansas City	2036	20	101

Commentary on Table 20: The deceptiveness of stats not carefully placed in various in-depth postures could be very apparent here, except to the unwary who might accept mere totals just at face value. The veteran clubs, early exposed to from seventeen to nineteen years of dead-ball influence, statistically are weakened by this attrition factor. The Twins and Kansas City never experienced this and the Orioles only twice. Note the closeness between the Indians's and Red Sox's totals. One heartening fact from a Boston point of view, not indicated in the table, is that the club holds the American League record—and it still is going strong—for the most consecutive years of over 100 team homers, 29, ranging from 1946 through 1974.

The following table, 21, is extremely informative to Boston fans, especially the implications of the last column:

Table 21
RED SOX CAREER HOME RUN LEADERS

Name	Total	Boston at Bats	Percent of Homers per 100 Times at Bat
T. Williams	521	7706	6.7
Yastrzemski	303	7759	3.9
Doerr	223	7093	3.1
Foxx	222	3188	6.9
Petrocelli	200	4748	4.2
Jensen	170	3857	4.4
T. Conigliaro	160	2898	6.2
Reggie Smith	149	3780	3.8
Malzone	131	5273	2.4
Stephens	122	2545	4.8

Back row, *left to right:* Speaker, Hooper, Cady, Mays, Gregg, Collins, Haley, Cooper, Leonard, Lewis. *Middle row:* Gardner, Janvrin, Foster, Corrigan, Hoblitzel, Gainer, Barry. *Front:* Thomas, McNally, Scott, Henriksen, Wagner.

BOSTON

Red Sox　　　　　　　　**1915**

BOSTON 1915 CHAMPIONS. In the full sweep of Red Sox history to date, this team is third only to the clubs of 1912 and 1946 in best seasonal record. Operating at a swift 101-50 ratio, vintage 1915 possessed both outstanding pitching balance and depth. Five bunched close together in victories; Foster, 19; Ruth, 18; Shore, 18; Leonard, 15; Wood, 15. This proved you can triumph without a 20-game winner. In Series, only three hurlers were necessary, each going the route without relief; Foster, 18 innings, Shore, 17, and Leonard, 9.

1915 RED SOX KEEP WORLD CHAMPIONSHIP IN BOSTON! Boston edged Detroit by 2 1/2 for pennant, then repulsed Phillies 4-1, in brief Series. In 1914, World Championship-bound Braves played Series games at Fenway, because the senior Bostons still were at Walpole Street where the crowd capacity was limited. 1915 saw the favor returned. New Braves Field was loaned to the Red Sox because of the larger seating capacity of the Gaffney Street grounds.

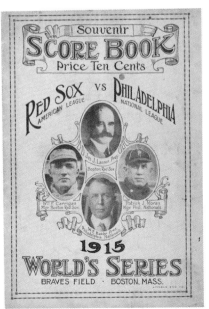

OPENING DAY AT FENWAY, 1916. The customary parade of ball players, frequently out of step, to the flagpole and salute to the Flag; uncustomary in that the current champions would be repeaters. Within the next year many major league players and thousands of other Americans would march to another drum beat, with greater precision, at various military training camps, then on to combat duty in the U.S. Armed Services. In this photograph, note the contrast of the contour of center field area with that of today's Fenway Park.

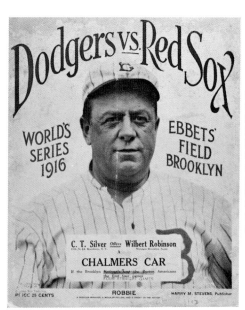

BROOKLYN BEATEN, 4-1, IN 1916 SERIES. Note the unrealized offer on this Dodger home program of a Chalmers car for Wilbert Robinson if his team won four straight. Scorecard publisher was Harry M. Stevens, Inc., also concessionaires at Fenway, 1916 to present. Toward end of program, under photograph of smiling President Wilson tossing out a first ball, Ty Cobb endorsed his reelection on November 7, following. Shore (2), Ruth, and Leonard, one each, secured Boston wins in this Series.

BOSTON WORLD'S CHAMPIONS 1916

Published by Baseball Maga-
zine Company, New York.
Top Row—Walker, Ruth, Gardner, Gregg, Jones, Henriksen.
Middle Row—Hooper, Leonard, Mays, Cady, Shore, McNally, Pennock.
Sitting—Hoblitzel, Scott, Carrigan (Manager), Agnew, Janvrin, Foster, Thomas, Lewis.
Photo by Photolane
Company, Chicago.

1916 CHAMPIONS. Another fine team, they edged Chicago by 2 for the flag. This photograph was one of the very best ever published in the old <u>Baseball Magazine</u>, a landmark for years. Despite sale-trade of Speaker early in season, Red Sox still had all-around team strength; best in fielding, second in pitching, fourth in hitting. Ruth was tops in League ERA, third consecutive season a Boston took such honors. Each winning Series share amounted to $3,900.

ERNIE SHORE (1914-1917). He was 56-32 overall, also with a Series record of 3-1. On June 23, 1917, Ernie became second Boston American to record a perfect game, and under most unusual circumstances. Ruth had started against Washington and walked leadoff batter Eddie Foster. After heated controversy with umpire Brick Owens over the calls, the irate Babe was ejected. Hastily warming up, Shore came in. Foster was caught stealing, then Ernie consecutively retired the next 26 Senators.

HUBERT "DUTCH" LEONARD (1913-1918). This lefty, later a millionaire, was an outstanding pitcher. Career 89-64, he had two no-hitters (St. Louis, 1916, and Detroit, 1918) and was 2-0 in Series. However, Leonard's greatest League achievement, which undoubtedly never will be surpassed, was an amazing 1.01 ERA in 1914. Although that season the Red Sox had 1-2-4 in individual ERA standings, it did not mean the pennant, as they trailed the hard-hitting, precise-fielding Athletics.

BOSTON RED SOX INFIELD, 1915-1917. One of their several team strengths was magnificent fielding. Boston led the League in team percentage six consecutive seasons, 1916 through 1921. Barry, in 1917, set an unsurpassed club record of 54 seasonal sacrifices, showing multitalent. In this period, contrary to today, Red Sox batters, rather than manager, used their judgment on whether to hit or take, or try hit and run with men on base. As Hooper expressed it, "each of us knew his own capabilities better than the manager and could do better with what he thought he could do and should do than the manager."

GEORGE "DUFFY" LEWIS (1910-1917). The regular left fielder for eight consecutive seasons, his greatest thrills were "leading both clubs in hitting, 1915 (.444) and 1916 (.353) Series." The 1912-1933 Fenway outfield included an embankment in his area, about ten feet wide, ten feet deep, rising somewhat precipitously to where it met the fence. Appropriately it was named "Duffy's Cliff" because of his alpine agility in maneuvering up, across, and down its difficult terrain. "Duffy" also recalled with pleasure his driving in Speaker with the only run in the famous Johnson-Wood pitching duel at Fenway, 1912.

"DUFFY" LEWIS

LARRY GARDNER (1908-1917). Another University of Vermonter, Larry was at third eight years, second in longevity there only to Malzone. In 1912 with Yerkes on third, one out, final Series game, score 2-2, bottom of tenth, Larry's poised bat, perhaps symbolic of a later great Boston conductor, Arthur Fiedler, struck winning note (outfield sacrifice fly). In 1916 Series, topped both teams in RBIs. Three times a World Champion, twice over .300, Gardner to this day is a deserved Boston hero.

101

WARTIME BASEBALL PRECEDENT ESTABLISHED. Although the United States went to war in April, 1917, professional baseball continued. However, next season's American League schedule was reduced from 154 to 128 games for each team, and World Series moved up to September 5. Red Sox were well represented in the Armed Services, especially in the Navy. Among those who served were Barry, Gainer, Hoblitzell, Janvrin, Leonard, Lewis, Pennock, and Shore. With liberal artistic license, <u>Sporting News'</u> cartoonist depicted 1918 Series interest of our sports-minded boys Over There.

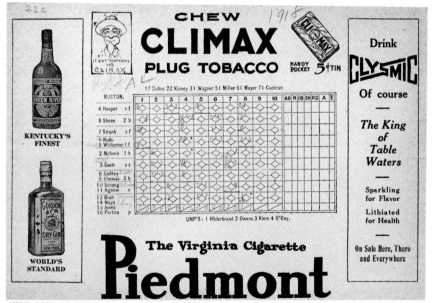

VERY RARE AT BOSTON 1918 SERIES SCORECARD. In immediate background, Boston (75-51) beat Cleveland by 2 1/2, a favorite margin, for the pennant, as their pitchers achieved 27 shutouts. This card records ending of Ruth's Series consecutive scoreless innings, begun in 1916, at 29 2/3 by losing Chicago. Record lasted until 1961 when Whitey Ford did even better. Red Sox comfortably won Series in six games.

GEORGE HERMAN "BABE" RUTH (1914-1919). Pitcher or batter? He was so good at both this question required Boston thought, particularly by team captain Harry Hooper. Applied mathematics furnished the answer; Ruth could pitch only every fourth day, but he could play the outfield every day. But before the solution was reached, the "Babe" really southpawed himself into Boston records; lifetime 89-46 and highest percentage (.659) for a lefty, 3-0 in Series, together with a long-lasting consecutive nonscoring innings mark.

CARL MAYS (1915-1919). He served Boston well, with his deceiving submarine delivery and 72-51 record. Only the fifth Red Sox to win over 20 games in consecutive seasons, Carl, on August 30, 1918, became second Boston to pitch and win two complete games on same day. He also hurled first opening day shutout. In championship 1918 Carl scored 8 shutouts and completed 30 games of his 33 starts, then won both his contests in the Series.

In 1915 we couldn't win the opening game of a Series—neither could we beat George Dauss, So Coming into Detroit Bill Carrigan our Manager in his meeting asked, "is there any pitcher here who thinks he can break this ginx? I spoke up and said, "If I Cant break it I will walk back to Boston", Bill said, "you are the Pitcher", my base hit in the ninth inning won it 2 to 1.

Carl, W. Mays.

One of the great anecdotes of Red Sox baseball, also a tribute to the wisdom of Manager Bill Carrigan, this was a fond memory of Carl Mays, undimmed by the great tragedy of Ray Chapman five years later.

103

WALLY SCHANG (1918-1920). This fine catcher is coholder with "Duffy" Lewis of highest Boston World Series batting mark at .444 (four for nine), which Wally achieved against 1918 Cubs. In 1918, each Boston winning Series share amounted to a very thin $1,102 each. Still a matter of controversy was denial of usual World Series Emblems to the Bostons because of the threatened strike before the fifth game.

WALTER H. SCHANG   R. R. 1, DIXON, MISSOURI   Sept. 12 - 1954

Dear Mr. Ellery Clark.

Your letter of Sept. 2 received and I must say it was very interesting — Still do I remember the 1918 World series — As I remember I hit 444 in that series. Was sure a great thrill. As I remember the greatest play I made in that series was when I got Charly Pick at the plate in a 2 to 1 game, prevented being the score — I threw in jutly ball. Agnes Stunk lives in Philadelphia — "Flynach Pa". you could probably get a program of 1918 series from any Boston paper. Would a Boston Post. If I had a picture I would send you one. I managed a semi-pro club at Grand Junction Colo this summer and caught all inning on my 64 birthday — and am sure feeling fine —

Sincerly
Wally

104

SAMUEL POND "SAD SAM" JONES (1916-1921). His very deceptive motion contributed to his 64-59 Red Sox record. Sam had League's best win percentage in 1918, three years later was best in shutouts, with five. Same season, with declining Red Sox, was club leader both in ERA and innings pitched. After that season Bush and he went to the Yankees as the ruination of the Red Sox continued apace. But Sam retained his fine opinion of Red Sox fans.

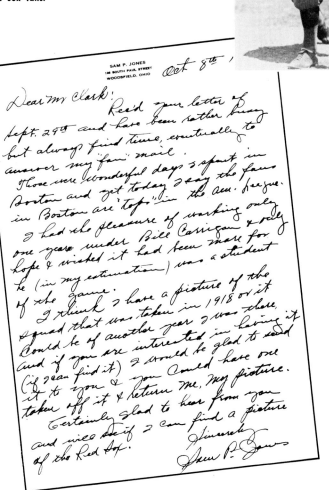

SAM P. JONES
100 SOUTH PAUL STREET
WOODSFIELD, OHIO

Oct 8th,

Dear Mr Clark:
Rec'd your letter of Sept. 29th and have been rather busy but always find time, eventually to answer my "fan" mail.

Those were wonderful days I spent in Boston and yet today I say the fans in Boston are "tops" in the Am. League.

I had the pleasure of working only one year under Bill Carrigan & only hope & wished it had been more for he (in my estimation) was a student of the game.

I think I have a picture of the squad that was taken in 1918 or it could be of another year I was there, and if you are interested in having it (if I can find it) I would be glad to send it to you & you could have one taken off it & return me, my picture.

Certainly glad to hear from you and will see if I can find a picture of the Red Sox.

Sincerely
Sam P Jones

105

EVERETT "DEACON" SCOTT (1914-1921). Dependable, durable, agile Everett, three times a World Champion, was sensational shortstop and veteran of eight great seasons. Best League fielder at his position for six consecutive years, 1916-1921, also twice tops in double plays. "Deacon" still holds Boston record for most consecutive games, 832. As to his nickname, baseball players of the period generally attached "deacon" or "parson" to the quiet, gentlemanly ones, of whom Edward Lewis was Boston's first, and Dan MacFayden, another.

LESLIE "BULLET JOE" BUSH (1918-1921). The origin of his nickname clearly related to his speed and his Red Sox mark of 46-39 was good, since Boston success rapidly was ebbing. He still holds club record for most seasonal 1-0 wins, five, in 1918, when he also led team in ERA. His banner 16-9 in 1921 led to the then inevitable; on to New York as they continued to acquire remaining able Bostons either by trade or purchase.

JOHN PHELAN "STUFFY" McINNIS (1918-1921). Former member of Mack's great Athletics' infield, "Stuffy" brought to Boston his well-known long stretch. In his final Red Sox campaign McInnis made only one error in 1,652 opportunities for a record .999 mark; during this he handled 1,300 consecutive chances without miscue. Years later he identified these accomplishments as "by far my happiest recollection for the Red Sox." Twice over .300, in 1918 Series he won one game with decisive hit, scored clinching run in another.

HOWARD EHMKE (1923-1926). Gentleman Howard remarked years later, "My most pleasant memory in those days was coming to Boston, where I was shown respect and kindness, which had not been my experience earlier with Ty Cobb in Detroit." He emerged as star righthander for a consistently weak team. Best season was 1923; he became first and only Red Sox to win 20 for a cellar team, also pitched no-hitter at Philadelphia, and just missed a second when on next appearance, at New York, first batter was awarded controversial hit. Then all the other Yankees were repulsed. The author, while a student in the mid-1920s, compiled approximate ERAs for the American League, 1901-1913, based on newspaper files in the Boston Public Library's periodical room. They are used in this book.

NO HITTER
BOSTON 4, Philadelphia 0
September 7, 1923

Doubles 67 1931

BOSTON RECORD
Year   B.A.
1930   321
1931   333
1932   281

EARL WEBB
MAJOR LEAGUE RECORD
HOLDER for DOUBLES
67 in 1931

Earl Webb

EARL WEBB (1930-1932). Outfielder Earl still is king of the doublers, and most likely will so continue. In 1931 he created a new major league, American League, and Boston record of 67 two-base hits, achieved in 151 games. In both 1930 and 1931, he was team leader in batting, homers, and RBIs. 1932 saw Red Sox as a club hit absolute bottom; 64 games off the pace, percentage of .279, and commensurate home attendance of 182,150.

IRA "PETE" FLAGSTEAD (1923-1929). Together with Ehmke he came from the Tigers, where his abilities had been underestimated. For seven seasons "Flaggy" delighted fans with diving, rollover catches. He had a very strong arm. His fondest Boston memory was "three times participating in a double play from my center field position in a single game, 1926." Four times a League leader, his best honor was in fielding percentage, .986, in 1927. Twice over .300, Ira made a still-existing club record for being their most-often-hit-batter, 11 times.

DAN "DEACON" MacFAYDEN (1926-1932). Bespectacled Dan from Somerville High soon gained prominence with a team that was on the bottom in six of his years. At 52-78, he did well. In 1929 he tied for League honors for most shutouts, with four. Two seasons later his 16 wins helped lift the Red Sox to sixth, only time in his career they were not last. Eventually Dan ended career with the Boston Braves, collectively winning 112 games for the two Boston clubs.

SOUVENIR SCORE CARD

Opening Day

New

Fenway Park

APRIL 17, 1934

HOME OF THE
BOSTON AMERICANS

OPENING DAY OF DOUBLE NEW DEAL! As this cover indicated, New Fenway Park, the old one torn down and a modern structure created, together with new and improved personnel, welcomed Boston fans to the renaissance. Rescuer and new president Tom Yawkey took over fourteen months earlier, on February 25, 1933, and quite literally salvaged what was left of the Red Sox. Inner program stated, "Boston must have another championship team." But a pennant would be elusive for twelve seasons. However, 1934 club rose to fourth, highest since the 1918 World Champions, and attendance jumped almost 342,000 over 1933, and 428,490 over 1932.

BILL WERBER (1933-1936). Primarily a third baseman, Bill brought his speed from the Yankees and became only Red Sox to lead League in stolen bases for consecutive seasons (1934-1935). These same years, he also topped team in homers. In 1935 Werber became first American Leaguer to crack four successive doubles in one game. Of all the still-active American League charter members, Boston is last in base stealing. Thus the exploits of Speaker, Werber, and Harper were well appreciated by Boston fans.

108

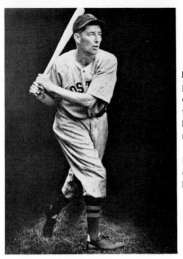

ROGER "DOC" CRAMER (1936-1940). An accomplished Philadelphia star, "Doc" brought his talented bat and center field abilities to Boston. Four times over .300, lifetime .302, he is 7th all-time best Red Sox hitter. Still holds team record for most seasonal at bats for left-hander, 661, in 1940. Recently he reflected, "Playing for a man like Mr. Yawkey was about the most important of all. He is a great baseball man and understands both the era that I played in and also today's."

RICK FERRELL (1933-1937). Although there was no Fenway Park echo, beginning in 1934 the announcer would say: "Batteries for today's game; for Boston, Ferrell and Ferrell." Brother-catcher Rick arrived a year before brother-pitcher Wes. Eddie Collins, Hall-of-Famer and Connie Mack's senior coach on the Athletics, in early 1933 became Yawkey's general manager and Rick was his first acquisition. He responded by batting over .300 and was five times a League fielding leader; percentage (2), putouts (2), assists (1).

WES FERRELL (1934-1937). A successful Cleveland veteran, Wes quickly became first Boston since Ehmke to break into 20-or-more victory group, repeated the following season to join Young, Dinneen, Wood, Ruth, and Mays as consecutive achievers. With a Red Sox mark of 62-40, Wes is last team member to hurl over 300 innings in a season—301 in 1936 and 322 for previous campaign. Holds club record (7) for most seasonal homers by a pitcher (excluding Ruth) made in 1935.

109

ROBERT MOSES "LEFTY" GROVE (1934-1941). Not since the 1901 arrival of Cy Young were Boston fans so excited when, in 1934, Grove took the mound for the Red Sox. Overcoming a bad arm and developing compensatory craft, Lefty won 105, lost 62, securing four League individual ERA titles and one percentage diadem. In 1969 was voted the left-handed pitcher on the Greatest Red Sox team. Counting his earlier Philadelphia victories, Grove reached the 300-victory plateau.

BOSTON RECORD

Year	Won	Lost
1934	8	8
1935	20	12
1936	17	12
1937	17	9
1938	14	4
1939	15	4
1940	7	6
1941	7	7
	105	62

LEFTY GROVE

"STRONG JACK" WILSON (1935-1941). Jack ended his Boston career at 67-67, first Red Sox with more than 50 decisions to reach final haven at even-keel position. Baseball nicknames, as expected, are descriptive. Other Red Sox ones include the talented and respected Harry Agganis, the "Golden Greek" (his sad, untimely death in 1955 was the third in Red Sox history, preceded by Chick Stahl's and "Big Ed" Morris's), Jumping Joe Dugan, Hawk Harrelson, Leaping Mike Menosky, Wiggles Porter, and Smoky Joe Wood.

BOSTON RECORD

Year	B.A.
1936	338
1937	285
1938	349
1939	360
1940	297
1941	300
1942	270

RED SOX RECORD HOLDER

Home Runs	50	1938
Runs Batted In	175	1938
Total Bases	398	1938
LEAGUE CHAMPION		
Batting	1938
Runs Batted In	1938
Home Runs	1939

JAMES EMORY "JIMMIE" FOXX (1936-1942). Primarily a first baseman, he still holds nine club records, and six times was League leader in seasonal stick performances. A member of the Greatest Red Sox team, Foxx's lifetime average of .320 placed him third, behind only Williams and Speaker. In 1938 he was selected League's MVP, first Boston so honored since Speaker won the predecessor award in 1912. Sooner or later "Jimmie" played every position for the Red Sox, including a one-inning hitless mound performance in 1939.

110

JIM TABOR (1938-1944). A third baseman, Jim was a crowd pleaser more at bat than in the field. He drove in 517 Bostons and hit 90 homers and was a League offensive leader in four categories. He also entered the League's fielding records in both directions. Once he had no opportunity either way when, in 1943, during a 12 2/3-inning game, not a single ball approached him.

JIM	TABOR
BOSTON	RECORD
Year	B.A.
1938	316
1939	289
1940	285
1941	279
1942	252
1943	242
1944	285

JOE HEVING (1938-1940). A highly successful reliefer (31-11), Joe was League's best, both in 1939 and 1940. Of the Bostons' between 25 and 50 career decisions, Joe's percentage is the most outstanding. In each of his Red Sox years he was second on club in ERAs. As in the careers of the Stahls and Ferrells, the Hevings also were a Boston brother combination, though not simultaneously; John was club catcher, 1924-1930, and an excellent fielder.

LOU FINNEY (1939-1945). Another Athletics' graduate, Lou was a competent, agile first baseman and outfielder. Over .300 for Boston career, in first season he was best in League pinch hitting; 13 for 40. His remarkable eyesight and quick, accurate judgment at the plate resulted in a very low 3 percent strikeout ratio in relation to his official times at bat. In unfair comparison, slugger Williams, though equipped with super vision, fanned nine percent of the time.

111

JOE CRONIN (1935-1947). In 1935, with Clark Griffith's necessary approval, Yawkey and Collins obtained him from Washington to serve as player-manager. Club's future obviously would be a considerable reflection of his abilities. This shortstop, four times over .300, became team's eighth all-time best batter, at even .300. Winning one pennant, Cronin managed Boston thirteen years, a record, later was elected to Hall of Fame and Red Sox Greatest Team. He served as American League President, 1959-1973.

CECIL "TEX" HUGHSON (1941-1949). Twice a 20-game winner (in 1944 League best in four pitching categories) and career 96-54, he hurled the 1946 pennant clincher at Cleveland, determined by Williams's inside-the-park homer. 0-1 in Series, "Tex" subsequently developed a bad arm. This factor, collectively applied, was a major reason for Boston's aborted hopes for pitching dynasty, perhaps multiple pennants in the next four seasons. Two "almosts" and well-remembered frustrations were the harvest.

DON'T LET US DOWN . . . . . By Gene Mack

BOSTON WORLD SERIES VICTORIES ENDED. Despite loyal, dedicated hopes of famed Gene Mack, Boston Globe artist, and the inspirational thoughts he developed in Boston on the morning of the deciding game at St. Louis, it was not to be. The Cardinals prevailed, on Slaughter's nonstop base running. Strangely, twenty-one years later, indicating history to a degree can repeat itself, teams again met with repeat result.

Commentary on Table 21: Most interesting! Foxx, Williams, and Tony Conigliaro were the club's three most frequent home run hitters and, on the average, the most dependable. Malzone, Reggie Smith, Bob Doerr, and Yaz were less likely. But any Boston fan knows statistical averages are not conclusive; any one of the above men, when at bat and with a long ball required, could and often did produce.

Conclusions. Home run records established through 1974 should hold up well in the future. Much depends upon the ball's resiliency, possible alterations in distances to fences and their height, perhaps an again lengthened schedule (which earlier permitted Maris to get ahead of Ruth in seasonal record). The relative quality of pitching and batting also will have to be considered. Some of the above remarks are pertinent to the explanation of why, in 1968, the total American League homer production was 1,104, whereas two years later it zoomed to a record 1,746 (of course there were two additional teams in 1970).

However, the very special home run thrill is unique for its partisans and has no serious challenger. For Boston fans, their present and future sluggers, though perhaps diminished in numbers, probably will come through an acceptable percent of the time, though the team's ultimate success more likely will depend upon the skills of their pitchers and all-around types of batters.

FIELDING:
IS THE HAND FASTER
THAN THE EYE?

Unlike in card tricks, in fielding the eye appears quicker, at first thought. Philosophically, only neutral-minded fans—and who would want to be in this noncommitted category—can fully enjoy the delights of great fielding (or pitching or batting) performances regardless of who may be the sponsor or beneficiary. Dedicated partisans are receptive only when these blessings of baseball life are created by and conferred upon their favorite team. At such times, what they see rapidly is followed by applause. To such fans, broadness of mind quickly reaches unyielding boundaries when some happening in one or more of these areas is detrimental to the selected idols. However, when such events occur and are not fatal to the local cause, the fan's qualified appreciation is increased, such as when viewing a rival's no-hitter and the outcome can be taken in stride. But win or lose, professional ball players over these many generations have continued to admire great plays regardless of who made them and what the influence was.

Unlike pitching and batting stats, those of fielding reflect performance in routine plays much more so than in the other two. On the average to date in the American League only thirty-one chances out of each thousand have not been acceptably handled, in the judgment of the official scorer. This is a remarkably small

114

error-of-commission factor. However, it is the degree to which errors hurt defenders that really counts. A damaging miscue setting up runs that do score is quite different from a harmless one that has no such effect. The following table provides the broad sweep of League fielding to date.

Table 22
AMERICAN LEAGUE AVERAGE
SEASONAL FIELDING PERCENT

1901-1919	1920-1941	1942-1960	1961-1974	Overall
.957	.969	.975	.978	.969

Commentary on Table 22: Should one be an incurable optimist, it is just a matter of time before perfection is reached, according to the rising peaks of the table. As the figures imply, the general and consistent improvement in fielding terrain and conditions, including much more effective gloves than the old-timers had, has been a factor in increased accuracy. Seasons 1964 and 1971 each produced the League's highest average fielding of .980.

Fielding is a peculiar domain, some of it explainable, some not. One always should expect the unexpected. For example, who would have predicted before game time on June 25, 1937, the Red Sox right fielder, Ben Chapman, would that day have seven consecutive fly balls hit within his grasp, for what would be a major league record, and still existing? Near the opposite end of the expectation spectrum is one that occurs frequently enough, though the odds are 9 to 1 against, to deserve comment. Why is it a player in the field who has just closed out an opponent's half inning with a brilliant play also is the scheduled first up when his club takes its turn at bat?

As is true also of batting and pitching, accepted fielding stats can be deceptive in the important area of omission. Fielders relatively slow of reflex and foot just cannot and do not cover the ground their more agile teammates or opponents do. Thus they do not have the opportunity of reaching more balls. Speedier, more aggressive fielders get to many of these, sometimes with error, but on the whole contributing more to their club's defense than the first type. A good example would be Ted Williams, who holds the second highest Red Sox outfield seasonal mark of .995, with just one error, surpassed in percentage only by Harrelson's perfect handling of 249 chances in 1968. Few would consider Ted a great fielder, especially after his serious shoulder injury.

Dipping into the fruit basket again to use the oranges and bananas reference once more, although team fielding, batting, and pitching percentage seasonal differences are somewhat impossible to compare and contrast, certain interesting results can be gained. For example, point variations between the League's seasonal top and bottom clubs within the categories of fielding and batting reflect much less difference in fielding, no doubt because of the prevalence of routine plays generally acceptably handled.

Table 23
LEAGUE CLUB AVERAGE POINT VARIATION
BETWEEN TOP AND BOTTOM TEAMS
IN FIELDING AND BATTING

	1901-1919	1920-1941	1942-1960	1961-1974
Fielding	.16	.12	.08	.09
Batting	.37	.35	.29	.27

Commentary on Table 23: On four occasions the teams have performed so evenly in fielding that the spread has been only 5, such as in 1943, 1952, 1953, and 1967. The greatest variation was 20, which occurred in 1907, 1908, 1910, 1911, and 1916. In contrast, batting's closest point spread was 17, in 1918, 1945 and 1973, whereas the extreme was 58, in 1911.

In the American League to date, since team fielding variations have been slight, it would appear that in an ideal equation for attaining a pennant, pitching and batting would be more important factors than fielding. Theoretically, we might agree that C (Championship) = EP (Excellent pitching) + EB (Excellent batting) + EF (Excellent fielding). Is such an equation realistic, when measured against the American League statistics of 1901-1974? In a few words—generally not—since this formula has been sustained only .027 percent of the time!

Table 24
PENNANT WINNERS AND
THEIR CONCURRENT TEAM LEADERSHIP
IN PITCHING, BATTING, FIELDING
OR VARIOUS COMBINATIONS

Club	Pitch.	Bat.	Fldg.	P & B	P & F	B & F	All 3	None
N Y	8	2	1	5	3		1	9
BOST	1	1	2	1		1		2
Det		5	1			1		1
Chi	2	1			1			1
Balt	1			1	1	1		
Clev	1						1	1
Minn		1						
Oak	1							2
Totals	14	10	4	7	5	3	2	16

Commentary on Table 24: Inquiry into the relevancy of pennant winners, and pitching, batting, fielding, and their various combinations, is quite in order. The Yankees have been almost equally adept at winning without benefits of firsts in any of these three categories, which they have done 9 times, as with associated fine pitching (8). Seemingly the Tigers slugged their way to flags on 5 occasions. Boston has shown good distribution and balance. But the overall statistics are even more revealing.

In sixteen seasons the American League champions did not stand first in any of these categories. Yet on 14 occasions they prevailed in pitching, another 10 times in batting and only 4 in fielding. In the various combinations, pitching also dominated, with 12 of the 15 hybrid leaderships. Once again it appears that pitching has been slightly more significant than batting, with fielding an obscure third.

Returning to fielding, great plays are a rarity. The most outstanding one for Boston dates back some sixty-three years when Harry Hooper made his catch in the deciding game of the 1912 Series. Even that was not the theoretical ultimate, because to achieve this, the fielding defensive gem would have to occur away from home and in the opponent's last time at bat, snuffing out potential tying and winning runs, as in the *Damn Yankees* plot. But routine plays also can be Boston remembered with pleasure; Rico Petrocelli's firm grasp of the Minnesota pop ended the Red Sox's 1967 regular season so happily.

Not as frequently as in batting, when the hitter has to make up his mind in a split second whether to swing or take, but applicable to outfielding, are associated considerations of quick decision and action. The great outfielders show a combination of anticipatory instinct, sharpened by knowledge about established hitters, and the ability swiftly to estimate where the ball will go as well as its speed, then taking off as necessary in swift sprint to the intercept point. The brilliant glove man has to be ahead of the developing situation. This quality, absent from accepted stats, is impressive to teammates, opponents, managers, coaches, and perceptive fans.

Another unreflected factor, true of all home teams, is the relative difficulty of playing the outfield, such as at Fenway. Since half the Boston games are there, the Green Monster is most important, testing fielders' anticipatory and experienced judgment in being at the right spot as soon as possible to play a rebound off the fence or correctly to time a last-moment leap, especially with a "tricky" wind in effect, to snare a fly ball just short of it. Center field also provides this problem, though not to so great an extent. Right field, besides being the sun field in day games, night or day provides many carom possibilities from batted balls bounding off the multiangled low fencing. Thus, the home team advantage of at least having more opportunity than the visitors to learn from experience.

Before commenting on great Red Sox individual and team fielding accomplishments, one final unrecorded influence should be mentioned. The effect of unscheduled errors in supposedly or actually routine situations may have a marked effect on the team's pitcher. He may be unemotional and stoic; he may be temperamental and subject to "blowing up" at critical moments. Intelligent opponents will grasp opportunity; perhaps expect wild pitches, or show more daring on the bases in order to draw an inaccurate throw from the mound.

In the list of Red Sox club seasonal individual record holders for fielding, 2 of the 6 were relatively journeyman players; with the team just a short while, but each had one splendid year with the glove. The other 4 are easily recognized as Red Sox greats, and certainly their abilities were not limited just to fielding achievements.

Table 25
RED SOX CLUB SEASON
INDIVIDUAL FIELDING RECORD HOLDERS

Name	Position	Percent	Year Made
Stuffy McInnis	1B	.999	1921
Bob Doerr	2B	.993	1948
Vern Stephens	3B	.978	1951
John Lipon	SS	.982	1952
Ken Harrelson	OF	1.000	1968
Mike Ryan	C	.992	1966

Commentary on Following Table 26: The really outstanding Red Sox seasonal and career fielders have been few, to do justice to the selective term. Based on the incompleteness of this table, seven Bostons are very prominent and all infield associated. Everett Scott, near peerless at short in his period, leads all the others, followed by hard-hitting, brilliant-fielding Bob Doerr and the incomparable Stuffy McInnis, who made only 1 error in 1,652 first-base chances back in 1921. Jimmy Collins, Lou Criger; Pete Runnels, and Rico Petrocelli, each gaining honors at 2 infield positions, and Rick Ferrell complete the group of Red Sox who led the League at least twice.

But what of the Boston trio of Speaker, Hooper, and Lewis, still considered one of the greatest all-time outfields? They do not appear in the percentage table. But in the more revealing and very useful category of outfield assists they were very prominent. Their quick catches or swiftly retrieved bouncing balls, unexpected by opponents, followed by accurate, fast throws to erase too daring base runners were frequent obituary notices of many when Tris, Harry, and Duffy responded. Their average number of seasonal assists, in years as Boston regulars, places Speaker at 28, Lewis, 22, and Hooper, 21. Among later Red Sox's proficients in this art have been Ira Flagstead, once a League percentage leader, who averaged 16 assists for his service as a Boston regular; Dom DiMaggio, Doc Cramer, and Carl Yastrzemski, each at 14; and Jackie Jensen, 13. Ted Williams, before his 1954 broken shoulder, averaged 10, then slumped to 4 after this.

Table 26
RED SOX LEAGUE SEASONAL
FIELDING PERCENTAGE LEADERS

First Base (10)			Third Base (7)		
LaChance	1904	.992	Collins	1902	.954
McInnis	1918	.992	Collins	1903	.952
McInnis	1920	.996	Vitt	1919	.967
McInnis	1921	.999	Kell	1953	.972
Todt	1928	.997	Hatton	1954	.966
Sweeney	1931	.993	Malzone	1957	.954
Foxx	1937	.994	Petrocelli	1971	.976
Goodman	1949	.992			
Zauchin	1955	.9951			
Runnels	1961	.995			

Second Base (7)			Shortstop (11)		
Barry	1917	.974	Scott	1916	.967
Doerr	1942	.975	Scott	1917	.953
Doerr	1943	.990	Scott	1918	.976
Doerr	1946	.986	Scott	1919	.976
Doerr	1950	.988	Scott	1920	.973
Runnels	1960	.986	Scott	1921	.972
Schilling	1961	.991	Rigney	1926	.969
			Rhyne	1931	.963
			Lary	1934	.965
			Lipon	1952	.982
			Petrocelli	1969	.981

Outfield (5)				Catcher (4)		
Strunk	1918	.988	Criger		1903	.979
Ruth	1919	.992	Criger		1904	.981
Flagstead	1927	.986	Ferrell		1934	.990
Oliver	1931	.993	Ferrell		1936	.987
Piersall	1956	.991				

The Red Sox as a team generally have fielded well, with nine League crowns, mainly achieved with the six-year streak from 1916 through 1921. With additional firsts in 1943, 1946, and 1950, the latter season also saw a new all-time Boston mark of .981. The team profiles are:

Table 27
LEAGUE TEAM FIELDING LEADERS, THROUGH 1974*

Team	1901-1919	1920-1941	1942-1960	1961-1974	Total
Chicago	6	3	6	1	16
Cleveland	1	2	6	1	10
BOSTON	4	2	3		9
New York	1	4	3	1	9
Detroit		4	1	4	9
Baltimore				5	5
California				1	1
Milwaukee				1	1

*Ties are included

Commentary on Table 27: Although Chicago has been a 16-time leader, only once has it been paralleled with a League championship. Club leadership has tended to go in streaks, much more so than the team ERA and batting averages. Boston had one of 6; Detroit strings of 4 and 3; Chicago, New York, and Cleveland each one of 3. The Red Sox have not been first in the above table since 1950, whereas Baltimore has shown exceptionally good defensive strength since its return to the League.

Conclusions on Fielding. Is the hand faster than the eye, now that the subconscious mind has been working on the question since the chapter's heading? It still is difficult to answer, perhaps impossible. But any great fielder appears to have an inbuilt impulse, sensing, alert system within his brain that almost instantly coordinates hand and eye and feet to the point where the skill and timing of the wonderful catch are recurring marvels every time it happens. It almost seems, even in this age of refined electronics equipment and systems, that the marvelous glove man has what amounts to a human homing system that frequently seems to doom in advance occasional very well-hit balls inevitably to be caught, however elusive they may seem to be. Consider this thought in advance of the next splendid outfield catch and see if it appears on target. At least agree to hope it will be made by a Red Sox!

BOSTON PROFILE IN CLOSE, UNCLOSE PENNANT RACES AND WORLD SERIES

"Take me out to the ball game . . . If they don't win it's a shame." Yes, indeed! These excerpts can be both optimistically and pessimistically approached. At each season's start, major league ball teams and their fans generally await the annual race with optimism. In the often pleasant spring season, conducive to happy thought and a renaissance in joyous anticipations, undimmed by recent past experience, there is little inclination to play the pessimist, to examine the worse than truth of the old contention, for every winner there is a loser.

In 1975 the American League positively has 11 potential defeated teams and only a single victor. The only fact in doubt until October will be the identity of the fortunate club. The baseball magnates are harsher in concept and practice than those representing professional football, basketball, and hockey, where in contrast relatively few clubs are eliminated as a long series of playoffs is customary. In baseball, you get the bad news early. But there is good news, for the American rather than the National League, at least from the record through 1974. The American pennant winners achieved victory in the World Series exactly 61 percent of the time to date; 43 Series won, only 28 lost. For various reasons, there was no Series in 1901, 1902, and 1904, which by statistical hindsight may have been very good National League judgment.

Obviously, pennants and World Series are won either by close or unclose margins. By strange coincidence, through 1968, after which the permanent Championship Series for the pennant was adopted, 24 races (35 percent of the total) were close and the other 44 (65 percent) unclose; and the World Series, through 1974, produced 25 close (35 percent) and 46 (65 percent) unclose results. Thus, more reliable than lightning, stats can and do strike twice in the same place.

What does the author mean by the terms, close and unclose? The former will include American League pennants through 1968 decided by 3 or fewer games; the 1948 one-shot, one-game championship playoff; flags since 1968 won by one game over the opponents in Championship Series; and World Series similarly decided. Unclose will include League pennants through 1968 won by at least 3½ games; Championship Series' triumphs by at least 2 games; and World Series titles similarly secured. One explanation quickly is extended to experts in simple mathematics; the author's won-lost figures do not balance. In certain close pennant fights, such as in 1908, 1920, 1940, and 1964, there were in each case 2 identified close losers, and in 1967 even 3.

Should the average reader not possess a photographic memory (no problem; who would consider himself or herself average?) and is not over sixty (any right-thinking person admits to not more than thirty-nine years), some surprises are in store in the various following tables and what they establish.

Table 28
CAREER PENNANTS

Team	Years in League	Pennants Won	Ratio of Pennants to Number of Seasons
New York	72	29	.402
BOSTON	74	8	.108
Detroit	74	8	.108
Chicago	74	5	.067
Baltimore	23	4	.173
Oakland	7	3	.428
Cleveland	74	3	.040
Minnesota	14	1	.071

Commentary on Table 28: Four currently active League teams have not won a single pennant between them. New York's past domination and career average is amazing; two flags for every five seasons. The Yankees also could and did produce semi-perennial winners; twice 5 straight; twice 4 straight; and three 3-in-a-rows. Psychologically that must have taken some toll of their opponents, as an immeasurable factor. There is some respectful whistling of current teams, hurrying through the tombstones of earlier New York accomplishments, as they contemplate the impact of Catfish Hunter's arrival on the 1975 playing scene.

Youngster Oakland has set the fastest pace of all and achieved League results that Cleveland has taken sixty-seven additional years to equal. Charter members Boston and Detroit have a good percent and total, while middle-aged Baltimore is commended on its performance, too. The other two charters, the Indians and White Sox, have not been graced with general success.

Table 29
CLOSE AND UNCLOSE PENNANT RACES
AND PERCENT OF VICTORY IN THESE

	Pennants Close		Unclose		Overall		
Team	Won	Lost	Won	Lost	Won	Lost	P.C.
New York	8	7	21		29	7	.805
BOSTON	5	2	3		8	2	.800
Oakland	2	0	1	1	3	1	.750
Detroit	5	5	3		8	5	.615
Baltimore	0	2	4	1	4	3	.571
Chicago	1	6	4		5	6	.454
Cleveland	2	6	1		3	6	.333
Minnesota	0	1	1	2	1	3	.250

Commentary on Table 29: Unclose losses occurred only in the Championship Playoff Series, which began in 1969. The tightest race was in 1948, a tie, with the Indians beating the Red Sox in a single-game playoff. In 1936, the Yankees established the biggest margin, 19½ games. Only the Red Sox and Yankees

did better than break even in the close preplayoff pennant strug-
gles. Oakland's 3 straight has been the longest streak since the
1949-1953 Yankees.

Table 30
CLOSE AND UNCLOSE WORLD SERIES

Team	Close Won	Close Lost	Unclose Won	Unclose Lost	Overall Won	Overall Lost	P.C.
New York	5	5	15	4	20	9	.689
BOSTON	1	2	4	0	5	2	.714
Oakland	2	0	1	0	3	0	1.000
Detroit	2	3	1	2	3	5	.375
Cleveland			2	1	2	1	.667
Chicago			2	2	2	2	.500
Baltimore	0	1	2	1	2	2	.500
Minnesota	0	1			0	1	.000

Commentary on Table 30: Note the Yankees's comfortable
Series wins on 15 occasions, proof of their powerful teams which
had winning streaks of 5 and 4. There was a slight American
League tendency to lose close Series to the National Leaguers
but in the comfortable ones the younger league prevailed, 27-10.
The Red Sox, of the charter clubs, has by far the best percentage.

Table 31
COMBINED TEAM TOTALS,
PENNANTS AND WORLD SERIES

	Won Close	Won Unclose	Lost Close	Lost Unclose	Totals Won	Totals Lost	P.C.
New York	13	36	12	4	49	16	.753
BOSTON	6	7	4	0	13	4	.764
Detroit	7	4	8	2	11	10	.523
Chicago	1	6	6	2	7	8	.466
Oakland	4	2	0	1	6	1	.857
Baltimore	0	6	3	1	6	4	.600
Cleveland	2	3	6	1	5	7	.416
Minnesota	0	1	2	2	1	4	.200

Commentary on Table 31: The Yankee stats require no additional comment! Once more the Red Sox are very well positioned. Valuable as these stats of the past may be, they cannot

illuminate the future. However, three teams, New York, Boston, and recent Oakland, have shown their many-dimensional strengths, quite indicative why they, of the actives, have stood out so much more than the others.

However, stats must be handled with care, as incomplete, and also the suspicion arises that too many of them may addle the brain. Moderation must be the byword. One of the most influential factors, not indicated in any of the preceding four tables, is one well known both to players, coaches and management of big league teams, but not confined to them. This is the "clutch" factor, one of the greatest of the immeasurables, though perhaps doctors, through blood pressure readings and stethoscopes and other devices and tests, in advance can determine who is and who is not susceptible beyond acceptable normal limits.

Stress and strain, frequently accumulative over a long period, such as was true of the League 1967 pennant race, exert the opportunity and necessity for players to make every best effort in the field and at bat. But opportunity and necessity often exert opposite pulls on the participants, regardless of their dedication and desire. Some react inspiringly and effectively, either maintaining their cool by controlling and channeling their adrenaline to best advantage, while others tighten both mentally and physically to the point where they are unable to produce their competitive best, good intentions notwithstanding.

So-called anticipated easy victory situations, whether actual or supposed, permit certain types of individuals and even teams to be relaxed to the point they will not have their best performances, but yet fairly good, which may not be sufficient on specific occasions. Some players and teams when anticipating unlikely victory may react detrimentally to their own performance. These influences—positive, negative, or mixed—will continue not to show in tables, but they will be influential. The serious practitioner of baseball (player, coach, manager) will be alert to try to turn these factors to his advantage, if possible.

Returning to the statistical tables, and looking ahead to the future during the annual playing schedules, mention is made of the late Cardinal Cushing's comment when he used to return to his Brighton, Massachusetts, residence after a brief out-of-town visit; "How's the team doing?" So concerned was he that he often said, "Don't bother addressing me by my church title. Just tell me what I want to know." Dedicated Red Sox and other League fans closely watch or listen to the daily standings on or in their favorite media. Every true fan, who also probably is unreasonable, believes his or her team should win its fair share in any season. But this turns out to be expectations at least of the pennant and preferably, to leave no remaining doubts, triumph in the World Series. The broad-minded fan is not particular about the margin of victory; one game in the decisive results is perfectly acceptable; it is not necessary to swamp the opposition.

So enthusiastic are some fans about the relative prowess of their favorite individuals and teams, often compounded when comparisons and contrasts encompass many unresolvable factors, such as widely different periods of baseball, characteristics of the ball, length of schedule, all day games or many night contests, that inconclusive arguments develop. The only results achieved by the participants is to strengthen already existing preferences and prejudices. Was Ruth a better home run hitter than Aaron? Would the 1954 Indians (111 victories) have beaten the 1927 Yankees (110)? Which would prevail, could the 1940 Tigers, 1944 Browns, and 1967 Red Sox meet under ideal conditions; each of the three had one shared achievement—League victory by a single game.

To the really reasonable Boston fan and historian, the team has done well, as shown in the preceding tables and discussion. If there is a relevancy between the past glories, including team and individual spirit and ability to win under pressure, then the hopeful Red Sox players and adherents of the present and future may anticipate more great seasons. But they will not come

JOHNNY PESKY (1942-1952) and the author. A great shortstop and third baseman, he is fifth all-time best Boston batter, at .313. In 1947 made a club record when an amazing 83 percent (172) of his 207 base hits were singles. First American Leaguer to score 6 runs in a 9-inning game. John served as Red Sox manager, 1963-64, then in 1975 returned as first base coach and batting instructor.

ROBERT PERSHING "BOB" DOERR (1937-1951). Unquestionably Boston's greatest second baseman. In thirteen distinguished seasons for the Red Sox, his only team, three times was over .300. During 1948 successfully accepted 414 consecutive chances. For career, 16 times a League leader in various categories afield. He returned to first-base coach the 1967 champions. His best memory; "When the fans of Boston gave me a night in '47 . . . a wonderful event in my years at Boston."

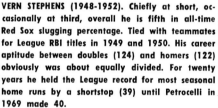

DAVID "BOO" FERRISS (1945-1950). He appeared destined to be one of Boston's greatest, but asthma, later arm trouble, cut him short, but not before he achieved 65-30, .684 mark, highest career percentage for a Red Sox with less than one hundred decisions. In pennant 1946, won his first ten, later twelve straight. Dave reflected, "Pitching in the World Series [0-1] gave me my greatest personal thrill, but my biggest disappointment came when we lost the seventh game."

VERN STEPHENS (1948-1952). Chiefly at short, occasionally at third, overall he is fifth in all-time Red Sox slugging percentage. Tied with teammates for League RBI titles in 1949 and 1950. His career aptitude between doubles (124) and homers (122) obviously was about equally divided. For twenty years he held the League record for most seasonal home runs by a shortstop (39) until Petrocelli in 1969 made 40.

WALT "MOOSE" DROPO (1949-1952). A huge first baseman, he acquired his nickname in part because of his Connecticut home town of Moosup. In 1950 he earned League leaderships both in RBIs and total bases. That season the League ball was the liveliest it has ever been, judging by team batting averages, with an average mark of .271, since season 1940.

130

DOM DiMAGGIO (1940-1953). He had ten full seasons of center field stardom. Eight times a League leader in various fielding categories, Dom was equally versatile at the plate, where he was superior six times in varied categories. Four times over .300, Dom is ninth in Boston batting, with .298. His greatest disappointment followed his game-tying double at St. Louis in 1946 final Series game. A pulled leg muscle restricted him to "watching from the bench instead of participating in that particular play." Reference: Walker's hit and Slaughter's run.

JOE DOBSON (1941-1950; 1954). Boston's fourth 100-game winner, he joined Young, Wood, and Grove, and completed 106-72 record. Dobson, unlike Hughson, frequently enjoyed advantage of having team score several runs for him. In 1946 Series, Joe was the Red Sox pitching standout; no earned runs in 12 2/3 innings, also ten strikeouts. Next year he won 18 games, his highest mark. Two years later, in relief, lost to Yankees in next-to-last game.

ELLIS KINDER (1948-1955). Both a fine starting pitcher and reliefer (91 saves), his career record was 86-52. Although Cy Young and he, by coincidence, each pitched eight seasons for Boston, Kinder, because of double duty, participated in 365 games, as against Young's 327. 1949 was a year of mixed emotions for Ellis; best in League for pitching winning percentage, yet was loser in pennant-deciding game. Despite his yielding only one run in his seven innings, teammates were blanked and eventually lost, 5-3.

BEST BOSTON ROAD STRATEGY?
With author's hearty endorsement, Manager MIKE HIGGINS suggests to TED WILLIAMS that he
hit another homer. Earlier, 1937-1938, Mike was Red Sox third baseman and in 1938 he made
12 consecutive hits, a major's record not surpassed. Higgins is second only to Joe Cronin in
years of Boston managership. TED WILLIAMS (1939-1960) is undoubtedly the last of the .400
breed, at .406 in 1941. Ted is Red Sox career best, at .344; won 6 League bat crowns and
topped the field over 40 times in various hitting categories, as well as being Boston career
leader in ten. As only a truly great can do, Ted celebrated his last official Red Sox at bat
with his 521st Boston home run.

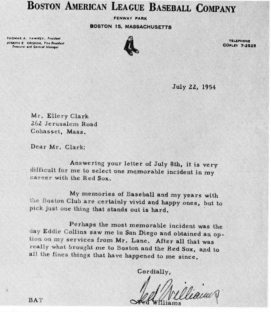

MY GREATEST MOMENT? Typical Williams's modesty prevailed when he wrote this letter, as well
as a deep realization that it all began when he was at San Diego. Williams caused strong
reactions among fans and writers, but this author has been in his corner. Although he declined
the opportunity to take advantage of the Williams's Shift, to this day he rightfully is acknowledged to be the greatest living authority on batting, who also is always willing to share
and impart his knowledge.

MEL PARNELL (1947-1956). At 123-75, Mel is winningest Red Sox southpaw and the fifth to join the limited century club. During 1949, led League in four pitching categories, though in Yankee series did not have his usual good days. Twice 20-game winner and 15 times a team hurling leader, late in career recovered from a broken arm. In his final Boston season, despite lingering influence of an ankle injury, Mel, on July 14, recorded a no-hit performance against the White Sox, at Fenway.

BILL GOODMAN (1947-1957). Frequently the regular second or first baseman, nevertheless in 1950-1951, also 1954, he was labeled utility. In 1950 Bill technically became first American League utility player to win the batting championship, at impressive .354. That year, club's bat percentage was .302, with six regulars over .300. He is sixth, at .306, in Boston all-time batting. During period 1946-1958, with exception of 1952, Red Sox had sustained cycle of first-division finishes, with attendance below one million in only one of these thirteen years.

JIM PIERSALL (1950-1958). Playing right or center field, Jim four times won League fielding honors. A good batsman, in 1953 he created a new club record of six hits in six appearances during a single game. Had 366 Boston RBIs and 66 homers. After overcoming serious personal problems, on return he combined hitting and dramatic abilities by responding with game-winning homer, while cameras made live shots for inclusion in his autobiography, <u>Fear</u> <u>Strikes</u> <u>Out</u>.

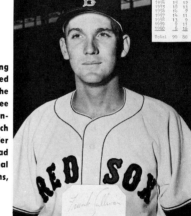

FRANK SULLIVAN (1953-1960). Tall and baffling styled (extensive wind-up and deceptive off-speed pitches), he finished at 90-80. Nine times the team's top hurler (distributed among the three major areas), in 1957 Frank had amazing control, averaging almost three strikeouts for each walk issued. Sullivan twice was a League leader and his favorite club, against whom he had marked success, was Baltimore. After his final season, American League expanded to ten teams, but still just one division.

JACK JENSEN (1954-1961). A fine strong-armed outfielder, he specialized in assists and double plays and was more prone than Williams to go after balls hit in the "gray area" of their fielding responsibility. Best in League five times; RBIs (3), triples (1), and stolen bases (1). Just before last game of season 1959 he announced his [temporary] retirement for the next year. In that contest, in his own words, "I hit a homer in the 13th to win it. That's called 'going down in a blaze of glory.'"

TOM BREWER (1954-1961). All too familiar, once again arm injury ended another Boston pitching career. At 91-82, his best season was 1956 when he gained 19 wins. Probably among the numerous causes of arm problems, the influence of Boston's occasional chill east wind (note Wise's experience in April, 1974) was and is a factor. The Boston hurlers, who performed at the Huntington Avenue grounds (Young, Gibson, Dinneen, and Tannehill), informed the author that they recalled no particularly adverse winds.

MIKE FORNIELES (1957-1963). A Havana product, he had a brilliant 1960 season; temporarily established American League and Boston record for most appearances in relief, 70, indicative of Boston's struggling seventh place finish. Mike also had 14 saves and team's best ERA for that season. He also made the ".400" club; 6 hits in 15 at bats.

PETE RUNNELS (1958-1962). An outstanding infielder, he became only the second Boston to win at least two League batting titles, which he accomplished in 1960 and 1962. Pete is tied for third-best all-time Red Sox hitter, at .320. Two years before his first bat crown, he was overtaken by Williams for the title on final day. A real sportsman, Runnels later evaluated this deprivation with the philosophic remark, "I enjoyed that more [than the two championships] because of the great competition he offered. He really closed fast that last week . . . wasn't he capable!"

IKE DELOCK (1951-1963). Which Boston pitcher had the longest service? Not Young (8), nor Grove (8), nor even Parnell (10), but Delock, with a dozen. Career 83-72, Ike had particularly rewarding seasons in 1956 (13-7), 1958 (14-8), and 1959 (11-6). In the latter year he probably better remembers his great bat exploit—only major league home run. After that campaign, in dwindling number of mound appearances, he was below .500.

FRANK MALZONE (1955-1965). A brilliant third baseman, Frank ten times was a League leader afield, particularly in double plays. He drove in 716 Bostons, hit 234 doubles, and 131 homers. His most pleasant memory was "playing in my first All-Star Game in 1957 which also was my first full year as a Red Sox player." Although there were several outstanding individual players in period (1959-1966), Boston was in a deep-down cycle, consistently in second division, twice next-to-last. Understandably, managers averaged a two-year tenure, if it can be called that.

BILL MONBOUQUETTE (1958-1965). Overall 96-91, he later concurred with British admiral Nelson's earlier remark that night was to his advantage in the 1798 Battle of the Nile. On the 164th anniversary of this action, August 1, 1962, Monbouquette warmed up for an evening game in Chicago. "I felt very loose for a cool night and I was popping the ball and had very good rhythm." He celebrated forthwith by pitching a no-hitter. A season earlier, Bill, also under the lights, fanned 17 Washingtons for a club record, not since approached.

DICK RADATZ (1962-1966). An outstanding reliefer for most of his career, he holds club record for total saves, 103, and finished at 49-34. 1963 saw Dick compile ERA of meager 1.97. Next season he made two Red Sox marks; most games, 79, and most games finished, 67. He appeared in exactly 48 percent of total Boston contests for that year, indicative of faltering starters, also 8th position of the team despite his valiant efforts.

EARL WILSON (1959-1966). Earl is proof positive that sometimes baseball statistics should be approached with extreme caution, and may be dangerous. For example, for his Boston years was 56-58, and in season 1962 he yielded 163 hits in 191 innings. But, on the night of June 26, 1962, before a tense and thrilled audience, he produced the first at-Boston under-the-lights no-hitter, against Los Angeles. However, his batting stats were very informative; almost one-quarter (.236 percent) of his Red Sox hits were homers. Excluding Ruth, Wilson holds club career-pitcher record for homers, 17, one more than Wes Ferrell.

DAVE MOREHEAD (1963 - 1968). Of course, no-hitters are unpredictable. Morehead was a modest 35-56 for Boston and in 1965 tied for League most seasonal defeats. But on September 16, before a fingers-crossed home crowd, he put it all together against Cleveland, achieving the still most-recent Red Sox no-hitter. Interestingly, and fully appreciated by Boston crowds, all but 4 of the 14 Red Sox no-hitters have been accomplished at home.

JOSE SANTIAGO (1966-1970). From Puerto Rico, popular Jose was a steady Boston winner in stretch-run of the great year, finishing at 12-4, with   dozenth victory in the vital next-to-last game against Minnesota. In Series, entered record book with first-time-up homer in opener. Next season, arm difficulties, unresolved by a later operation, terminated his career at 33-23. He remains a great Red Sox hero for his obvious contributions.

GARY BELL (1967-1968). Although Boston was eighth in 1967 ERA stats, it was very close; only a .022 difference between the first three contenders and Red Sox bats made that up. Acquired from Cleveland in early June, Gary became instant starter; 12-8 for season, 23-19 lifetime. Boston won championship with record lowest percentage of .568, because of four-team struggle. Few would have predicted victory with eventual wins of their "big four" reading 22 (Lonborg), 12 (Santiago), 12 (Bell), and 8 (Stange).

KEN "HAWK" HARRELSON (1967-1969). Though just passing through Boston, the "Hawk" was a great favorite out in right field, and helped in the 1967 surge. But the next year he astounded his critics and delighted his fans by being chosen Player of the Year by the authoritative Sporting News. Leading the League in RBIs with 109, Ken, in addition, fielded faultlessly, topping the American League and creating a new club record of 249 chances accepted without lapse. Happily, in 1975 the Hawk returned to Boston as an announcer.

138

NO ENERGY SHORTAGE HERE! Wildly enthusiastic Bostonians ripped sleeve and buttons off Lonborg's shirt as the photographer accurately portrayed him as center of attraction. "Yaz" on the periphery meanwhile took cautious route, via visitors' dugout, to Red Sox dressing room, where soon thousands of congratulatory telegrams would adorn the walls. The Red Sox had won the 1967 League Championship!

Pennant Is Ours!

TOP BILLING FOR 1967 AMERICAN LEAGUE CHAMPIONS. The city's newspaper response to the achievement of "The Impossible Dream." In a very real sense their team included millions of American fans pulling for the questing Red Sox diamond-knights. The reach of Boston ballplayers' determination and abilities had grasped the dream, outdoing Cervantes's fiction hero. The frequently trite and overused phrase "desire to win" in 1967 American League play had become an energized reality.

JIM LONBORG (1965-1971). His lifetime mark of 68-65 is not indicative of the high as well as tragic points in his Boston years. As much as any one single player could, he pitched Boston to the 1967 pennant, with additional League honors as Cy Young Award winner and most strikeouts. He allowed only four hits altogether in his two Series triumphs. But, on following December 24, he tore two ligaments in left knee as result of ski-slope accident and never regained his former brilliance.

MIKE ANDREWS (1966-1970). Carefully coached by Bob Doerr, Mike had best seasons in 1969 and 1970, though in pennant 1967 his .263 was very capable for a second base rookie. In Series, third among the Red Sox, at .308. Same year was League's most prolific in sacrifices, with helpful 18. In 1969 earned tenth place in League batting at .293. Interesting and unusual, his RBI total steadily increased during Boston tenure; 40-45-59-65.

RAY CULP (1968-1973). After outstanding first two seasons, at 33-14, Ray increasingly suffered arm troubles which an operation in 1972 for a torn shoulder tendon did not cure. Despite this, he was 71-58. Red Sox, following the flag in 1967, in the next four years were way off the winning pace, averaging some 19 1/2 games behind. The club's annual victories in the same period were within remarkably narrow range of 87, high, and 85, low.

WILFRED "SONNY" SIEBERT (1969-1973). At a final 57-41, affable "Sonny" had exceptionally effective first three years, averaging 15 wins annually. He was later hampered by ankle injury and arm trouble. In period 1968-1973, team developed upward-plateau graph in annual finisher of 4-3-3-3-2-2. In 1972, Detroit beat club out by half-game for division title, next season Baltimore won by eight.

GEORGE SCOTT (1966-1971). Variously at first and third, George had most League putouts, also double plays at initial sack in his first two seasons. Also contributed to pennant, with .303, fourth best, and 171 hits, tied for fourth among League batters. The "Boomer's" career offensive marks were quite inconsistent; .245-.303-.171-.253-.267. Overall for Boston hit 105 homers, 107 doubles, 390 RBIs. In Series, fielded 73 chances without error.

REGGIE SMITH (1966-1973). A switch-hitting outfielder of relatively greater bat than fielding prowess, he twice was League best in doubles, 1968 and 1971. Twice over .300, Reggie produced for Boston 149 homers and 536 RBIs. In Series, Yaz, Rico, and he hit fourth-inning homers in sixth game, a record. Smith coholds with Jensen the club seasonal record for most homers by a center fielder, 25. For various reasons he was traded to the Cardinals at end of season 1973.

TOM HARPER (1972-1974). An experienced out-fielder, his 1972 arrival returned necessary base speed to Boston. In 1946-1971 period, team had annual average of only 42 steals, with extreme lows of 18 in 1964 and 20 in 1951. Tom immediately supplemented 141 hits with additional 47 percent of walks, both tactically helpful in stealing 25 bases. In 1973 he led League with 54, eclipsing Speaker's old club mark of 52, set back in 1912.

BILL LEE (1969-   ). Expectantly, a forthcoming ace lefty of the pitching staff, and currently in 11th place in all-time Red Sox hurling percentages, he enjoyed a fine 1973; third in League ERA (also third best by a Boston in last fifteen years) and 17-11. As somewhat infrequently occurs, Bill began as a reliefer, then was added to starters as others faltered. 53-37 to date.

CARLTON "PUDGE" FISK (1969-   ). In 1972, his initial full season, catcher "Pudge" became first American League unanimous selection for rookie of the year, also tied for League lead in triples. To date, in his own words, "My greatest on-field satis-faction was participating in 1972 All-Star game. I can remember how nervous I was, yet so proud and filled with emotion." Fisk holds team seasonal homer record for a receiver, 26 in 1973. Seriously injured June 28, 1974, in a base-line collision, and out for the rest of season. Suffered broken bone in 1975 spring training.

AMERICO "RICO" PETROCELLI (1963-   ). "Rico" at both short (2) and third (1) has been League's best fielder. Also holds Boston seasonal record for most homers by shortstop (40 in 1969) and third baseman (28 in 1971). His most thrilling experience to date came during "the sixth game of the 1967 Series because I hit two home runs and we won the ball game." He is among club career top ten leaders in six batting departments.

LUIS TIANT (1971-   ). Cuban-born, genial, mustachioed, cigar-smoking Luis in 1971 was considered by many baseball "experts" to be all through, but not by Boston strategists. He responded with revived arm and deceptive turnaway motion of torso, topped League in 1972 in ERA with magnificent 1.91. Next season he became first Red Sox 20-game winner since Lonborg, and fashioned 22 more in 1974. Currently 58-39 for Boston.

TONY CONIGLIARO (1964-1970; 1975). Closing on an heroic note, everyone is pulling for Tony C. to win a berth as DH in 1975. Brilliance combined with misfortune have been his characteristics. On August 18, 1967, he suffered very serious eye damage when struck by a pitched ball, but gallantly returned as a regular again two seasons later. As quoted in the New York Times, April 15, 1975, Tony said: "I pray to the patron saint of miracles, Saint Anthony. I think that in the position I'm in I should explain this to people who need to come back." Youngest major leaguer ever to hit 100 homers, he has parked a total of 160 for Boston to date. He holds club record for most seasonal homers for a right fielder, 36, in 1970, and also stands 4th in club career slugging percentage. Come on, Tony!

CARL YASTRZEMSKI (1961-   ). Truly the complete durable ball player, in 14 Boston seasons outfielder-first baseman "Yaz" to date has been League offensive best 18 times, including three each in batting, doubles and runs. He identifies his outstanding Red Sox satisfaction with 1967, because as a team member "We won the pennant, also my greatest individual moment since . . . I won the Triple Crown." He has made 2,267 Boston hits, 303 homers and 436 doubles as well as providing excellent, sometimes brilliant, fielding. Six times over .300, he also is in club career top leaders for ten departments, standng first in career at bats, with 7,759, through 1974.

by inheritance nor by formulae. They will have to be gained by self-made Bostons, with coach and manager help and guidance, able to put it all together, as did many of the old-time and some of the not-so-old-time Red Sox. Their names will vary, but the challenges, opportunities, and obstacles will remain much the same as they have been in the past.

For the established Red Sox players to come, less relative interest in annual or long-term salaries and in off-the-field enterprises and more actual on-the-field attention to baseball would help. No doubt player reaction to this comment would be most adverse. But this is one active-years' advantage the early great Bostons possessed, in times when ball players had little opportunity, outside their meager salaries in the sport, of building financially for the future. Perhaps the pendulum will swing a little the other way, thus helping the actual playing performances and at the same time not being injurious to the players' very valid concern with their own futures, once their spikes and gloves are laid aside. With reasonable fortune, some of these tools of the trade, as in the past, eventually will represent Boston in Cooperstown. These closing thoughts all are pertinent to the future hopes for Red Sox pennants and World Championships, whether they be achieved with relative ease or only after the closest competition.

MYSTIQUES OF
BASEBALL STATISTICS

The compilers of baseball stats are acknowledged, dedicated, sincere people, supported by public approval. They gather, print, and distribute certain accepted data, useful though incomplete, about individual players and teams; who, what, when, and where. They do not establish either cause or effect. To a genuine purist in the field, an accepted stat is an accepted stat. Sometimes they can save certain people money, such as $25,000. Oakland owner Charles O. Finley, in salary arbitration, as recently as February 19, 1975, appears to have won his case against Captain Sal Bando, of his champion Oaklands, primarily because he effectively cited Bando's 1974 decline in 14 of 16 accepted stats. Bernie Carbo, a .249 Red Sox hitter, by similar arbitration, was repulsed—again presumably by the influence of statistics—in his bid for $50,000 for his forthcoming 1975 labors in behalf of the Boston cause. Carbo will improve in 1975. Ask Mr. O'Connell!

The author strongly holds two statistical opinions; one is a reality, the other probably just a Quixotic dream. There is a positive relevancy of accepted stats to both the present and the future. But a try should be made, highly controversial as it would be, to compile some new statistics and publish them for public information. These suggested new stats would give a fairer, in the sense of more complete, profile as to the actual and relative merits of ball players in their various categories; pitching, batting, fielding.

Among the baseball set, regardless of such other worthy subjects as the currently staggering economy, the nation's recommended best attitude toward Israel and the Arabs, what we should do about Cambodia, personal health and success in love and business (certainly not incompatible, as their own stats reveal), statistics continue to hold a forward position. Any real fan has at least something to say, if not astound listeners, on the subject, often trivia limited.

To these, certain questions and their believed illuminating answers always are ready for instant display to the unsuspecting. For example, which American League team holds (proudly we assume) the record for the highest percentage of games won for a 6th place team? Obviously, the 1926 Detroit Tigers, at .513! Ready for another? Who made the most wild pitches and when, in his first major league game? Of course, the unfortunate Tom Seymour, who better had remained in bed. On September 23, 1882, representing the old Pittsburgs (then spelled that way) in the National League, he uncorked five. The saddest few words of all were recorded in the balance of this record item; "his only game in the majors." Fortunately there is a vast wealth of useful nontrivia for management, player, and fan.

In 1969 (revised edition, 1974) appeared *The Baseball Encyclopedia,* a monumental volume of research, corrections, and additions, second to none in its field, jointly produced by The MacMillan Company and Information Concepts Incorporated. There also are many other reliable sources of considerably older heritage, such as the annual *Official Baseball Guide,* C. C. Johnson Spink, publisher, his many annual and occasional other paperbacks and his "Baseball Bible," the erudite *Sporting News,* founded March 17, 1886, and a family concept and production.

Right now, in the realm of restrained fancy, because of increased research interest, statistics locators, armed with their baseball equivalent of Geiger (electronically or otherwise, especially otherwise, this name recalls Gary Geiger, a Red Sox from 1959-1965) counters, may be sensing new potential sources. Should such strikes be made—and the use of the term could be symbolic and punnish—and assuming they be accepted by management-player-fan, it could influence players most. A salary increase could very well develop from the assessment of new data, revealing hitherto unrecognized and unpublicized abilities of certain players. On the other hand, it could work against certain accepted stars and their prominence in accepted data, which might be weakened by the harsh light of broader illumination.

The prominent, esteemed weekly columnist of *The Sporting News,* Mr. Leonard Koppett, in his 1967 *A Thinking Man's Guide to Baseball* (E. P. Dutton & Co., New York), included a chapter entitled, "Figures Often Lie." Leonard reached the irrefutable conclusion, "Standard baseball statistics count only certain selected items . . . ignoring the effect of other equally countable items that are obviously related." Some reasons why this is so must include the tradition support of the accepted ones and the disturbing possibility to management that more inquiring, penetrating standards of player measurement might deface idols, to the anger of these and their fans. Quite possibly a .240 hitter might be proven or greater all-around value than one positioned at .285.

The author presents a partial list of factors. *General ones* applicable to individual players for comparative purposes would include: is he baseball intelligent? Does he perform well under stress? Does he learn from mistakes or repeat them? Is he injury prone? Is his personality an asset to the team, average or unbearable? Does he continually hustle? Is he past his production potential or under it? Does he take care of himself away from the park? *For pitchers:* Does he have a good assortment? Control? Deceptive change of pace? Restrict the good hitters? Keep his weight and legs in shape? Field his position well? Possess a good defensive motion and adequate arm, to keep base runners close? *For catchers:* Does he call pitches well and does he make an efficient team with both experienced and rookie moundsmen? Is he alert for opponents' base moves or surprise batting decision? Does he have a strong, accurate arm? *For batters:* Does he have quick, discerning eyes for bad balls and change of pace? A low strikeout ratio? Does he hit in stress situations? Has he speed and can he bunt well? Can he hit to various fields; and is he a spray- or long-ball type of hitter, or capable of both? *For fielders:* Does he cover adequate ground? Does he handle the ball well and avoid careless errors? Has he speedy legs and a good arm? Does he throw to the right base at the right time, and also field ground balls well? Does he avoid critical communications failures when two or three are gathered together in quick pursuit of a difficult fly or ground ball?

As in umpiring, many of the above factors are within the judgment-call range, with considerable room for debate if not strong disagreement. But any alert contemporary club is well advised to pay attention to these factors, both relative to their own players and opponents, especially those who may be eyed for a trade. Certainly the purpose of all this would not be to transform baseball into one huge clinical laboratory, but to evaluate the whole man, not just the partial one.

Returning to accepted stats, what is the relevancy of Red Sox team pitching, batting, and fielding to their final standings? Admittedly, these are soundings into only four of x possible deeps, but are believed sufficiently representative and capable of producing acceptable conclusions.

Table 32
COMPOSITE OF RED SOX ANNUAL FINAL POSITION AND
THEIR TEAM POSITION IN ERA, BATTING AND FIELDING

Final Standing	No. of times in position	ERA	Batting	Fielding	Totals
1	8	5	12	9	34
2	11*	7	13	11	42
3	11*	6	13	9	39
4	12	14	9	9	44
5	6	9	5	5	25
6	5	7	7	8	27
7	7	7	4	10	28
8	12	11	11	8	42
9	2†	5	0	3	10
10	0	1	0	1	2
11	0	1	0	0	1
12	0	0	0	1	1

*In six-team Eastern Division, beginning 1969 (2nd twice, 3rd, four times)
†Ten-team League, 1961-1968

Commentary on Table 32: Although providing a broad spectrum, clearly the information in this table does not reflect patterns and trends, the latter being an important feature of practical analysis. However, in general the club's final position has been a little above average; pitching below average; fielding above average. But batting has been commendable. Now, inquiring into the yo-yo Red Sox years, to compare extreme opposites, the following:

Table 33
COMPARISON, RED SOX BEST YEARS
(FINISHED FIRST OR SECOND)
AND WORST (SEVENTH OR LOWER)

Year	01	03	04	12	14	15	16	17	18	38	39	41	42	46	48	49	67	72	73
Finish	2	1	1	1	2	1	1	2	1	2	2	2	2	1	2	2	1	2*	2*
ERA	2	1	1	2	1	2	2	2	2	3	5	5	3	4	4	4	8	11	5
Batt.	4	1	4	2	3	2	4	3	6	1	1	1	1	1	3	1	1	3	2
Fldg.	2	2	2	2	2	3	1	1	1	6	3	4	2	1	2	2	9	8	3

*Six-team Eastern Division

Year	06	07	22	23	24	25	26	27	28	29	30	32	33	43	45	60	62	63	64	65	66
Finish	8	7	8	8	7	8	8	8	8	8	8	8	7	7	7	7	8	7	8	9	9
ERA	8	5	6	8	4	8	8	7	7	7	3	8	4	7	8	8	9	9	9	9	10
Batt.	6	8	8	8	8	8	8	8	8	8	8	8	5	7	2	3	4	2	1	2	4
Fldg.	8	4	8	8	6	8	4	7	2	7	4	7	8	1	4	7	5	6	8	9	9

Commentary on Table 33: In the nineteen good seasons, Boston almost half the time showed remarkable consistency in the four categories, with stats for 1903, 1912, and 1946, the most convincing of their superiority. 1972 marked the greatest variation, wherein the adverse ERA record undoubtedly was one reason the club (5th in ERA) was edged out by Detroit for the division lead. 1967, when they won, was marked by strong batting and down-side average pitching and fielding. Consistency is the general mark of both good and bad teams, as Boston well knows by experience.

Twenty-one bad seasons produced their own sad Red Sox

pattern, especially in 1922-1932. Note in the last seven of the listed unfortunate years ERA proved more influential than first-division batting in affecting the final standing, a trend repeated in the 1964-1974 period.

Occasional good team pitching, as in 1924 and 1930, was unable to offset woeful batting, in which the Bostons were 13 and 24 points, respectively, under the League's average mark. Progressing to another interesting area, the years of unusual variation —10 out of 74, thus 13 percent—deserve examination.

Table 34
RED SOX UNUSUAL VARIATION SEASONS

Year	11	30	36	44	67	68	69	70	71	72
Finish	5	8	6	4	1	3	3	3	3	2
ERA	1	3	2	8	8	8	9	8	10	11
Batt.	4	8	7	1	1	3	3	2	5	3
Fldg.	6	4	4	3	9	3	10	12	5	8

Commentary on Table 34: In the first three cited years, good pitching did little to elevate the team as it tended to seek its own batting level. But in the other seven, strong hitting helped overcome relative weak pitching. Thus, in 70 percent of the marked variation years, batting was a fairer yardstick than pitching in measuring Red Sox's finishes and causes thereof. But enough of the past, the most recent years and their obvious trend is of greatest practical Boston significance.

Table 35
RECENT RED SOX TRENDS, 1964-1974

Year	64	65	66	67	68	69	70	71	72	73	74
Finish	8	9	9	1	4	3E	3E	3E	2E	2E	3E
ERA	9	9	10	8	8	9	8	10	11	5	7
Batt.	1	2	4	1	3	3	2	5	3	2	4
Fldg.	8	9	9	9	3	10	12	5	8	3	3

Commentary on Table 35: In the first three seasons team finish and ERA standing were closely associated, then in the next two batting was more a determinant. But in the most recent six, the annual finish is compounded by the fact that the League has been operating in two six-team divisions; thus the Red Sox eastern position must in some way be equated with the western teams. Perhaps multiplying their standing by 2, then subtracting 1 would be a reasonable approximation of the old one-division League. At any rate, in these most recent six years the club's divisional finish has been much closer to their batting than to their pitching profile. Their hitters have averaged a third position and pitchers only eighth. 1973 Red Sox management was well aware of this and attempted remedial action, by trade and purchase. But in 1974, for unpredictable reasons, the effort was at least a one-year failure, despite the best of intentions and action.

Once again the expected/unexpected uncertainties of baseball emerged just before game time on August 24, 1974. At that moment Boston possessed what appeared to many to be an unassailable Eastern Division commanding lead of seven games, despite serious, lingering injuries to Wise, Fisk (still pursued by misfortune, his right forearm was broken in 1975 spring training) and Marichal. Thirty-eight games later, after the fatal combination of a Red Sox skid of 14-24 and sustained hot streaks by both the Orioles and Yankees, Boston finished a distant third, seven games behind and their lowest percentage since 1966.

For the American League division leaders, comparative statistics explained at least a good part of the finish. Once again good pitching proved more important than good hitting, good health superior to torn cartilages, injured shoulders and backs, and the teams able to win close, crucial games went to the top. Late-slumping Boston in the final weeks lost more because of lack of timely hitting than weak pitching. Ten defeats were by low scores; 0-1 (3), 1-2 (3), 2-3 (1), and 1-3 (3). Eight of eleven games were lost to the other contenders; Baltimore (1-5) and New York (2-3). In the long decline, Red Sox batters statistically were averaging 3.3 runs knocked in per nine innings, insufficient production to offset 3.7 runs yielded per nine innings.

ERA for the ultimate leaders proved very influential. Oakland, the eventual continuing World Champions for the third straight season, was best at 2.95. Baltimore, division winners in the east, second at 3.27 and New York third, at 3.31. Boston was a distant seventh, at 3.72. Not unfairly bending statistics a bit, the ERA superiority of the Orioles (0.45) and Yankees (0.41) overcame the Bostonian team batting edge of 8 and 1 points, respectively. Considering all the above cited facts, the Eastern Division's top finishers were consistent with the believed general applicability of the respected statistics.

However, statistics can be used to prove or disprove many theses, particularly when deliberately cited or omitted in an attempt to present a biased conception. California, with the League's poorest record in 1974 (68-94), nevertheless could extract some cold statistical comfort in finishing fifth in ERA (3.52) and ninth in batting, some seven points ahead of Champion Oakland. But, as usual, the only statistical table of ultimate primacy is that which shows the percent of games won.

Unfortunately for Boston, season 1974 proved the continuing viability of Robert Burns's poetic and enduring philosophy of the well-laid plans of man not in themselves being guarantees of victory, because of unpredictables and variations. Red Sox Executive Vice President Richard O'Connell, disappointed by Boston's eight-games-back 1973 finish, when many, including Eddie Kasko, had anticipated success, concluded that new pitching strength and a different manager might provide the solution. 1973 statistics were encouraging; team ERA was fifth, best showing since 1957, and their famous batting continued, second in the League.

By well-intended purchase and trade in the off-season, five experienced pitchers came to Boston, with a previous season's combined record of 60-57. But Wise (16-12) and Marichal (11-15) were expected to be very effective newcomers to the

League. The group finished 1974 with a limping 33-37. Wise (3-4) and Marichal (5-1) were disabled more than able; the former's last pitching decision was on July 6, the latter's on August 11. First-string catcher Fisk was out for the season on June 28, following a leg injury and necessary surgery. Only Tiant (22-13) of the veteran Bosox came through, as Lee and Moret slumped to a combined 26-25 record.

Statistical Conclusions on Red Sox Team Position, Pitching and Batting.

1. A general truth for success whether statistical or otherwise: capable pitching + adequate batting + adequate fielding. They have to be timely, especially in close, important games. Victories by massive runs mean little, except to swell certain stats. And statistics are only averages; they are not intended to and do not apply to specific situations.

2. When Boston seasonal pitching and batting effectiveness is noticeably different, as has been in seventeen (65 percent) of these twenty-six years, the club's final standing has been closer to that of the hitters rather than pitchers and their hurlers generally have been less effective than their batters. Thus, a Red Sox endorsement of the time-honored claim that pitching is about seventy percent of the game. Interestingly, in 1974, Oakland preceded its successful World Series defense by achieving the greatest variation in League history; first in ERA, 11th in hitting. If their success had been the other way around, probably the Orioles would have been League champions. But the A's made their runs count, thriftily defended by fine pitching, as the Orioles and Dodgers very well remember.

3. Baseball stats (both accepted and recommended) can and should be intelligently studied. They indicate in most cases when a trend or pattern is established, how a club can improve. Whether it will or not, as in the case of the unfortunate 1974 Red Sox, is another matter.

In the haze of statistical mystique, the reader is entitled to a capsulated overview of just how well the Red Sox have done, 1901-1974, in relation to the other senior American League clubs. The following table presents club placements, on the basis of frequency, in League individual and team leaderships in various important categories, with the totals indicating, as in a cross country race, that the lowest possible score (first place = 1 point) is desirable. Most readers probably would have anticipated the correct exacta; Yankees first, Red Sox second. But even a Middle Westerner would be hard put to distinguish between the Tigers and Indians for third.

Table 36
CLUB PLACEMENTS

Club	Individual Pitching			Batting		
	ERA	%	Wins	Champ.	HR	Total
New York	3	1	2	4	1	11
BOSTON	3	2	5	2	2	14
Detroit	5	5	3	1	3	17
Cleveland	2	4	1	3	4	14
Chicago	1	2	4	5	5	17

	Team							
	ERA	Batt.	HR	P.	W.S.	Fldg.	Total	Overall
New York	1	3	1	1	1	3	10	21
BOSTON	4	2	2	2	2	3	15	29
Detroit	5	1	4	2	3	3	18	35
Cleveland	3	4	3	5	4	2	21	35
Chicago	2	5	6	4	4	1	22	39

Key: P = ranking in number of pennants won
W.S. = ranking in number of World Series won

Selected Comments: These stats are in general conformity with accepted baseball philosophy. The Yankees were best in pitching, close to the top in hitting. Boston's superior place in batting contrasted with a low posture in pitching. The Tigers showed a sharper discrepancy than the Red Sox. Chicago's good mound and fielding ratings were dragged down heavily by feeble hitting. Cleveland appeared slightly more effective on the mound than at the plate. This compilation does not create more statistical fog; on the contrary, reasonably clear and faithful team images are evident.

4. Ball players, with or without the use of stats, win or lose pennants and World Championships. No two seasons are or will be alike; varying influences, including the unpredictable, will continue to challenge the best abilities of athletes and management. If things go wrong, do not blame it on the computer! Return to the philosophy of Willie Keeler and broaden his commentary from "Hit 'em where they ain't!" to include "Hope they hit 'em where we are!" If nothing else, it would put the favored team's (Red Sox) responsibility more equally on batting and fielding. Their pitchers, by inference, would be encouraged to try to make the opposing batters hit balls directly at their fielders, also to administer a reasonable number of strikeouts. Come to think of it, theoretically this appears to be an invincible formula for Red Sox victory, especially if it could be copyrighted and all rights reserved! Only one problem remains; transforming the formula into successful reality!

RED SOX HALL OF FAME: THE FIRST SEVENTY-FOUR YEARS

Back in 1936 the first members were elected to the Baseball Hall of Fame, Cooperstown, New York. In 1969, under Boston Red Sox auspices, New England fans voted on an All-Time Greatest Red Sox Team, one player for each position except pitcher, where they chose one right- and one left-hander, for a total of ten players. Although this concept and its implementation was highly commendable, since no previous large-scale effort had been made to select the best, it did have some practical weaknesses.

For example, the major fault lay in disregarding mortality figures. The fans of 1969 necessarily included very few of the original ones, who, if they had been teenagers back in 1901 and were still alive in 1969 would have had to have been about eighty-six, considerably older than the average life span. Thus the otherwise commendable equal vote process recorded few ballots on behalf of the early Bostons, with exceptions of the illustrious Cy Young and Tris Speaker. All the others on the selected team were from the Yawkey years, certainly a fine tribute to the owner's great efforts, also those of his staff, to assemble the best possible Red Sox clubs. Yet this was to the general neglect of the great teams of 1903-1904 and 1912 through 1918. The 1933-1969 years obviously were the ones most familiar to the fans who participated in the election and their preferences of course reflected this.

However, now that seventy-four years of the club's history have passed, it is an appropriate time to make an attempt to nominate as impartially and fairly as possible a more representative team, both in periods of Boston history and in number of honored players. It does not seem presumptuous to begin an individual club Hall of Fame as a natural development from the National one. An existing and probably not correctable inequality of the National Hall is that many players of excellent qualifications, especially those of the early years, unless they were absolute standouts, like Wagner, Cobb, Johnson, and Mathewson, or a few later selected by the Centennial Commission or the Committee on Old-Timers, were passed over. There also have been recent allegations of New York-biased voters. No selection process will please all and injustices will occur, despite the best of intentions. Those just below the cut-off line, whether past, present, or future players, felt, feel, or will feel in their hearts and minds at least regret at having lost out in a close one.

The author has talked with many former ball players on this touchy subject, both to those accepted and rejected. He is impressed with the respective pleasure or disappointment they have quietly shown and expressed, dependent on the outcome. He hopes there will be no great personal displeasure with his list. No intentional favoritism has been exercised. As in other areas of life, there will be mingled emotions and some disagreement.

The adopted ground rules for selection include the following. Outstanding achievements, considering both career and individual season performances; arbitrarily, at least three years as a Boston regular; choices were made strictly by position, both in the infield and outfield; two were chosen for each, except there were twelve pitchers; also utility players and designated hitters deserved inclusion and received it. This selector has one direct judgment asset; he has watched the Red Sox play ball for fifty-six years. Here are the members:

BOSTON RED SOX HALL OF FAME, 1974

First Base	Foxx and McInnis
Second Base	Doerr and Runnels
Third Base	J. Collins and Gardner
Shortstop	Cronin and E. Scott
Utility Infielders	Goodman, Pesky, Malzone, Petrocelli
Left Field	T. Williams and Yastrzemskl
Center Field	Speaker and D. DiMaggio
Right Field	Hooper and T. Conigliaro
Utility Outfielders	Lewis, Jensen, Flagstead
Designated Hitter	Cramer and Reggie Smith
Catchers	Carrigan and R. Ferrell
Pitchers	Young, Dinneen, Wood, Foster, Shore, Ruth, Grove, Ferriss, Hughson, Parnell, Kinder, Tiant
Team Captain	Hooper
Team Manager	Carrigan

Commentary:

1. *Representation.* There are some noticeable differences between the above list and the 1969 group. Thirty-seven not just ten are honored. Although Tebbetts does not appear in the larger list, at least four outstanding additions have been made: Jimmy Collins, Harry Hooper, "Duffy" Lewis, and Dom DiMaggio.

2. *Captain Hooper.* In the author's considered opinion only he deserves this honor. His common sense, great baseball experience, insight into what best should be done in practical situations, fine temperament, ability to gain and hold the admiration of teammates and opponents alike, and longevity of demonstrating these qualities are only a partial list of his many talents.

3. *Manager Carrigan.* After consulting a great many former Red Sox as to their views on the merits of a number of managers and making a judgment on these, the author is convinced, as

in the case of Hooper, there is an equal agreement about who should manage. Bill Carrigan is the choice. Admittedly he had great personnel playing for and with him. He had many of the same attributes as did Hooper, but one in particular was characteristic of Carrigan himself. This was his application, as the situation and/or individual best required, of tough or gentlemanly conduct. Babe Ruth quickly learned the determination and physical force of Carrigan. The Babe did not challenge his authority again. In the other type of approach, as the quoted letter from Carl Mays (whom few people understood) in the pictorial section has shown, Bill would call an occasional meeting for a very important purpose. In that particular reference, Carrigan sought an aggressive, confident pitcher who assertively would volunteer for an assignment in which teammates previously had failed, and then go out and accomplish it. Mays did.

4. *Philosophic Dreams.* What a team or teams the Boston Hall of Fame theoretically could put on the field, assuming each was in his prime and unrealistically dismissing reality (differences in age). The author would not claim an undefeated season for them, such as the original Cincinnati Red Stockings achieved in their early days, but believes they would do the old city and area proud in confrontations with other American League Hall of Fame teams, should these be created.

5. *Visual and Audible Retention.* The author vividly recalls with unending delight the occasional old-timer games in Boston when he was a teenager. The old Boston Nationals and Boston Americans played a couple of innings each time. He still can hear the cheers, not gone with the general wind but preserved in memory's oral history, when the best-of-the-best picked up glove, bat, or ball and went out there again, as aging, applauded heroes. Young, wearing his Boston uniform; Lewis, Speaker, and Hooper trotting out to the old familiar places; Speaker with his still powerful, graceful stance and swing at the plate, all are wonderful memories. There will be more in the future, and

younger fans will be able to see some of the great players before their time, still retaining elements of form and grace that mark the outstanding athlete, active or retired.

6. *Conclusions.* These old-timer games of past, present, and expected future complement the regular season, annual All-Star Game and World Series, thus furnishing a bond from yesterday to today to tomorrow, and all that it implies. To the spirit of all this the author most respectfully dedicates this selected Boston Red Sox team, always open to players of the present and future. May other historians choose their favorite clubs and state philosophies about them. The times are right; 1975 brings the seventy-fifth anniversary of the American League, and that of charter member Boston. Historians, take your positions!

RELEVANCY OF PAST
RED SOX BASEBALL HISTORY
TO THE PRESENT AND FUTURE

Believing the future begins right now, but looking over his shoulder at the constructive past, the author regards Boston baseball history from the practical side; what can it do or suggest to present and future players, managers and coaches, and front-office management? As in the case of military and naval history, so, too, with baseball. Too many professionals or alleged professionals have not bothered, or been required, to become familiar with the constructive lessons and experiences of their winner or loser predecessors or contemporaries. Japan's faulty submarine strategy in World War II is an excellent example. Learning indirectly of someone else's first-hand experience with trial and error is a less bruising way to acquire knowledge than by personal hard knocks. There is no claim that historical familiarity with the past can solve most problems that may arise in the future, but it teaches one to be observant, analytical, and practical. Whether by reading, conversation, correspondence, listening to taped interviews, viewing photographs and motion pictures or other devices, current owners, managers, coaches, and players, if they were that interested, could add to their effectiveness. This is particularly true in 1975 when win still continues to be the name of the game, financially influenced by the sagging economy and perhaps gates, compounded monetarily and otherwise by many star players making every effort to gain huge contracts, as did Catfish Hunter.

Some statistical interpretations and conclusions, based on millions of bits of data studiously gathered from the past and recent past, are worth only a limited amount, consistent with the cold facts of what was rather than what will be. Annual guides, encyclopedias, and record books are treasure troves less for the trivia seeker than for those more seriously and practically oriented. But these sources offer no direct key to the uncomputerizable intangibles which in themselves are the mysterious leaven from which great performances can rise. These will continue to elude and defy disinterested researchers, especially those who lose themselves in a world of detached factual minutiae, those who lack the desire, qualifications, opportunity, and experience of leading athletes in serious, challenging competition. In the intangibles lives an underrated responsibility of the manager, frequently neglected by the general public, sometimes even by management, unless the team fails.

Routine plays, tactics, and procedures can well be handled by coaches, including the dubious but venerated practice of having batters in pregame hitting be serviced easy pitches totally unlike what they will face, including change of pace, in the actual game. The manager is directly responsible, according to management, stated or implied, for at least the following qualities of the team: desire, confidence, consistency, achievement close to full capability, grace under pressure, concentration, ability to face the unexpected, taking advantage of the breaks, learning quickly from mistakes, endurance (including the medical responsibilities of club trainer and physician), good team communications and cooperation, not underrating the opposition, and hustle. Most players, coaches, and managers can recite these terms in dull monotones, from high school or earlier days on up. Few can or will bring them into full play.

On the other hand, the tangibles deserve equal attention.

There is no substitute for basic talent, enhanced as it can be by the above qualities. Pennants are won with good players, not mediocre or poor. The Red Sox victories of 1903, 1904, 1912, 1915, 1916, 1918, 1946, and 1967 were no accidents, no lucky achievements. Their 1922-1932 failures just as easily can be explained. Tangibles reinforced and blended with intangibles produce the best, with the partial exception of the current three-time Oakland World Champions. Although they play wonderfully effective ball on the field, off it (including in the locker room) they are well known for personal differences, including with management. But that is gaining success the difficult, not the ideal, way. In contrast, Larry Gardner, writing on the solidarity of the great Boston teams of 1912, 1915, and 1916, remarked in 1974, "On Sundays, when at home, the team frequently went to Revere Beach for a day's outing and we really enjoyed ourselves. In reality, we were a big family." No doubt today many will consider this a naive, old-fashioned characteristic in an era long passed and never to be reproduced, but it is one that pleased many of the old champions and helped their on-the-field cooperation in a period of American history when family unity probably was greater than it is now.

Four conclusions may be reached in the area of tangibles-intangibles for Red Sox attention. Some of the stats, as usual, must be regarded with a wary eye.

First. Excellent pitching is the single most important necessity for success. But the familiar statistics do not reveal what really was and is important; who kept or will keep men off bases or from scoring in crucial innings and games? General averages are just that and do not tell who came through or did not when a game was in a clutch environment. However, from the revered stats there is much for Boston selective regard and application.

For instance, in the seventy-four American League championship seasons to date, the winners have been either first, second, or third in team ERA on 67 occasions (90 percent of the time); in these, 33 firsts and 24 seconds, convincing indication that good seasonal pitching has been characteristic of most champions. But runs win games, and the object is to outscore the opposition.

Second, batting. In these seventy-four seasons, the champions have been hitting leaders exactly 28 times, and second 19 times, another indication of general statistical offensive prominence of the winners. If pitching is not quite of prime quality, effective batting often can pick up the slack, as the Red Sox did in 1967. Once again it is the combined factor of timely defensive and offensive play.

Third, fielding, subject to the same qualifications as to timeliness of good or bad plays. As already indicated, team seasonal fielding averages do not appear to have been of too much significance. But in a crucial moment, yes! In the 1912 World Series, Hooper's earlier brilliant catch for Boston and Snodgrass's later error both were serious misfortunes for the New York team.

Fourth, but not necessarily assigned to this place, the intangibles. Team determination in 1914 of the Boston Braves quickly comes to mind. Also in September, 1967, the dedication of many of the Red Sox to the motto, "We've got to win," with the tremendous moral support of millions of fans inside and far outside Massachusetts. Many people still fail to recognize adequately the fourth, because it is not and probably will not be a published statistic. Probably the luck factor should also be included in this category; the batted ball fair or foul by proverbial inches, or the ball beyond or within grasp by the same small margin.

Only the successful blend of these four factors and qualifications can produce a championship team. The preceding sentence compacts about as much baseball wisdom as is possible in a few words.

Further developing the importance of the manager, the Red Sox's seventy-four-year history provides much material for examination, thought, and conclusion. Their first one, also a brilliant contemporary third baseman and thus player-manager, Jimmy Collins, had served the Boston Nationals in the five previous seasons, establishing a fine reputation as leader, fielder, and batter. Persuasive, he brought key teammates over to join the then new Boston Americans, who also were bolstered by other valuable additions. With a fast start, the team was 2-3-1-1 in first four years, then age and other baseball liabilities overcame them. Manager Jimmy plummeted from a 14½ game winner in 1903 to a narrow 1½ game victor in 1904, then to 16 behind the next year and finally 45½ in arrears in 1906, when he was relieved by Chick Stahl.

However, with intimations of success by 1909, in 1912-1918 came the period of excellence: four World Championships and twice League runners-up. Bill Carrigan, manager for part of 1913 and all of 1914-1916, firmly established himself as the greatest Red Sox leader of all time, combining brilliant athletes with very effective direction, suitable to the various types of personality with which he had to deal and not by unvarying application. By admission of his own players, then and later, he was both a student of men and of the game, and could apply his wisdom equally, coordinating the two, as it should be.

But not even the most brilliant Red Sox manager can do well with a lack of talent, further compounded by the team's then financial near-poverty, such as in the grim period 1922-1932. In fact, from 1925-1932, the closest Boston finished to the champions in any one season was 43½ games, in 1928, under Bill Carrigan, who unwisely came out of retirement. The nadir was in 1932, when Shano Collins and Marty McManus could pilot their charges only to within sixty-four lengths of the champion Yankees. Joe Cronin, with one winner, had the longest tenure, thirteen years, and also played a brilliant shortstop most of that period.

In seventy-four years Boston has had thirty-one managers, some of them repeaters. A number of these, such as McCarthy, Boudreau, Higgins, and Kasko, had both talent and player problems. Their collective comments would be worth a fortune. Unhappy relations between management-manager-players, often increased by insufficient success, sometimes in the past affected by certain antagonistic writers, have been causes of heavy Red Sox managerial traffic. Management in Boston as elsewhere sets their own standards; if and when the manager in their judgment is noticeably below these, off he goes, infrequently to return. Dick Williams still is a discussion topic.

One philosophic thought, based on Red Sox research, is worth mention. Win or lose, much or little talent, their players did their best at the time, and generally developed no lasting regrets, being able to place their baseball experience in a proper perspective relative to their entire lives. There appears to be a lasting common bond of friendship and admiration among ballplayers in general, exceeding that of fans, a strong indication of an enduring baseball brotherhood in the best sporting sense. The March 1, 1974 death of "Laughing Larry" Doyle, famous second baseman of the old New York Giants, is an excellent example. With the kind permission of Captain Harry Hooper, of the early Red Sox, excerpts from his letter to the author, dated March 12, 1974 (Harry died on December 18, 1974), are quoted:

I was saddened at the news of Larry Doyle's death. When I heard of his passing I already had written a plaque card [Hooper's individual Hall of Fame card] to him. I had been thinking about him because I knew he had been in bad health for some time. After greetings and well wishes, I wrote: 'To Larry Doyle, the man whose line drive in the final game of the 1912 Series should have been a home run. If I hadn't caught the ball the Giants would have won in 9 innings, and Larry Doyle would have been the hitting hero

of the Series. With his great career record it is possible that
he instead of me would have been in the Hall of Fame.'

... I went back to attend an Old Timers' game at Fenway
some years after the 1912 Series. A number of National
Leaguers were there whom I had never met. Duffy Lewis,
then Road Secretary of the Boston Braves, introduced me.
Then we came to another group, including Doyle, and
Duffy inquired, 'Larry, you remember Harry Hooper don't
you?' 'Remember him?' replied Larry, 'How in hell could I
ever forget him!'

No doubt this element of mutual respect and kindness will
continue in Red Sox and associated major league history. May
both the dedicated and casual reader of this book share in his
or her own way in whatever this collation of photographs, facts,
memories, emotions, interpretations, and conclusions may produce. As in other aspects of this human condition, baseball provides limited success to many and great success to but a few.
But all those who at one time or another have donned the
Boston uniform did their best, regardless of the outcome, and
for this they have enriched the sporting history of the city. Their
spirit and dedication hopefully links the Boston baseball past,
present, and future.

Victory comes to only a few and of course is not everything
in life, in the opinion of most people. But as an early and un-
identified student of athletics once commented, "It sure beats
defeat!" May the Red Sox present and future both have more
friendly than ominous skies! May hoped-for improved Boston
fortunes in some way relate to new and reexamined concepts,
various stats and their interpretations, and especially to the
intangibles and tangibles by which the author has tried to show
the relevancies of Red Sox past failures and successes to both
their present and future. Boston baseball history, its interpretation and applicability, is significant only if it still lives and can
assist those who want to gain from its lessons and encouragement.